European Repo

EUROI
POCKE. BUUK

CW01394519

1990 EDITION

Volume 1
France, Holland,
Belgium, Ireland,
Netherlands

Series Edited by Phil Hodgson
Neil Webster
Philip Wormald

ISBN 0-947773-17-7

© **1990 Metro Enterprises Ltd., 48 Southcliffe Drive, Baildon, Shipley, BD17 5QX**

FORWARD

This book is the first volume in a series of three pocket size books intended to be a guide to the locomotives of the railways of Western Europe. The other volumes in the series will cover the following countries (subject to alteration between the volumes):

Volume 2: Denmark, Norway, Sweden, Finland, West Germany.
Volume 3: Austria, Greece, Italy, Portugal, Spain, Switzerland.

Provided that the series is well received it is our intention to produce the series on an approximately annual basis and perhaps later expand the scope of the volumes to include multiple unit vehicles and also other information useful to British Enthusiasts when travelling abroad.

Readers comments are welcome to amend, update and improve the series. Photographic contributions (preferably black & white prints)are also invited for the other volumes in the series and also for future editions of this volume. These should be sent to the following address:

Metro Enterprises Ltd.,
312 Leeds Road,
Birstall,
BATLEY,
West Yorkshire,
WF17 0HS.

All comments and photographs will be acknowledged.

Phil Hodgson, Neil Webster & Philip Wormald.   April 1990.

INDEX

INTRODUCTION

Under each country heading are listed the locomotives of both the national railway system and any other private railways, but excluding industrial and tourist lines and preservation sites. Depot allocations are given where available or appropriate, with a listing of the codes used appearing under each individual railway heading. (Z) shown alongside a locomotive number or allocation indicates that the locomotive was stored at the time of going to press. The storage location may in some cases be a location other than the home depot of the locomotive as shown. A full list of other depots, works and stabling points for each railway is also given, but in the case of the latter the information is based on observations only and may therefore be incomplete.

For each locomotive type brief technical details are given in metric units with their approximate imperial unit equivalents in parentheses. Weights are quoted in metric units only (1 tonne = 1.016 tons). Codes are used to indicate the various builders/manufacturers/constructors and these are common throughout this volume and appear in a table at the end of this introduction. Abbreviations used for metric and Imperial units etc. are as follows:

ft	feet
hp	horsepower
in	inches
km	kilometres
km/h	kilometres per hour
kW	kilowatts
m	metres
mph	miles per hour
mm	millimetres
rpm	revolutions per minute.

For each country information regarding "Railrover" and similar tickets is given to assist the enthusiast in planning visits to Europe. All prices quoted are the latest available at the time of going to press and reflect the position in the spring of 1990 unless otherwise stated. Further details regarding tickets and fares may be obtained from the offices of the relevant railways or their agents at the addresses shown.

COVER PHOTOGRAPHS
Front: SNCB no. 5153 heads a line-up of members of this class at Hasselt depot on 15th July 1989 . *(Dale W. Fickes)*
Back: SNCF BB7284 arrives at Aix-les-Bains with a Talgo set bound for Barcelona on 13th June 1983. *(Dale W. Fickes)*

GUIDE TO LOCO/EQUIPMENT BUILDERS

The following abbreviations are used for builders in locomotive class headings.

ABC	Anglo Belgian Corporation NV.
ABR	Ateliers Belges Réunis SA.
ACEC	Ateliers de Constructions Electriques de Charleroi SA.
AFB	Société Anglo-Franco-Belge des Ateliers de la Croyère.
Allan	N.V. Allan & Co.
Alsthom	Société Générale de Constructions Electriques et Méchaniques Alsthom.
B & L	Brissonneau & Lotz.
Baldwin	Baldwin Locomotive Works.
Billard	Anciens Établissements Billard & Cie.
BM	Baume et Marpent SA.
BN	Constructions Ferroviarires et Métalliques. (formerly La Brugeoise et Nivelles SA).
BREL	British Rail Engineering Ltd.
CAFL	Compagnie des Ateliers et Forges de la Loire.
Carel et Fouché	Établissements Carel & Fouché SA.
CEM	Compagnie Electro-Méchanique.
CFD	CFD Industrie.
CGC	Compagnie Générale de Constructions.
CIE	Coras Iompair Éireann. (now Iarnród Éireann)
Cockerill	Cockerill-Ougrée SA. (now Cockerill Mechanical Industries SA).
Decauville	Société Nouvelle Decauville-Aîné.
De Dietrich	De Dietrich & Cie.
Deutz	Klöckner-Humbolt-Deutz AG.
Fauvet-Girel	Établissemnets Fauvet-Giral.
Fives-Lille	Compagnie de Fives-Lille pour Constructions Méchaniques et Enterprises.
GM	General Motors, La Grange Works, Illinois, USA.
Heemaf	Heemaf NV.
Henschel	Henschel und Sohn GmbH.
Jenbacher	Jenbacher Werke AG.
Jeumont	Forges et Ateliers de Constructions Electriques de Jeumont.
Jung	Arnold Jung Lokomotivfabrik GmbH.
MaK	Krupp MaK Maschinenbau GmbH.
Moyse	Établissements Gaston Moyse.
MTE	Société de Matériel de Traction Electrique.
MTU	Motoren- und Turbinen-Union Friedrichshafen GmbH.

MV	Metropolitan Vickers Ltd. (now part of GEC).
Niv.	SA Les Ateliers Metallurgiques de Nivelles.
Oerlikon	Société Oerlikon.
SACM	Société Alsacienne des Constructions Méchaniques.
Schneider	Société des Forges et Acieries du Creusot, Usines Schneider.
Séchéron	SA des Ateliers de Séchéron .
SEM	Société d'Electricité et de Méchanique (Charleroi).
SEMG	Société d'Electricité et de Méchanique (Gent).
SEMT Maschines	SEMT-Pielstick (formerly Société des Études des de Thermiques.
Siemens	Siemens AG.
SLM	Schweizerische Lokomotiv und Maschinenfabrik.
Voith	J.M. Voith GmbH.
Werkspoor	Werkspoor NV.

Top: NIR BREL/Hunslet built 101 class no. 101 passes Adelaide whilst working the ITG "Bangor Belle" railtour on 10.09.89. *(J. M. Allen)*

Bottom: NIR General Motors built 111 class no. 113 stands at Dublin Connolly after having arrived with a working from Belfast Central. *(D. W. Fickes)*

NORTHERN IRELAND

Northern Ireland Railways (NIR)

Gauge: 1600 mm (5 ft 3 in).
Route Length: 330 km.

Depot & Works

Belfast Central Service Depot (located at Belfast York Road). Workshop attention to 111 Class locomotives is occasionally made at the Inchicore (Dublin) works of Irish Rail.

Railrover Information

7 Day All-Line Runabout Ticket: Available April to October. 7 consecutive days unlimited standard class travel on all NIR services. Prices: £25.00 Adult, £12.50 Child (5-16).
8 Day Irish Rover Ticket: Issued in conjunction with Irish Rail. 8 days unlimited standard class travel on both NIR & IR services within a fixed 15 day period. Prices: £55 Adult, £27.50 Child (3-15).
Tickets & Details: NIR, InterCity Travel Centre, 17 Wellington Place, Belfast, BT1 6GB (Tel: 0232 230671). 8 Day Irish Rover Ticket ia also available from IR (qv).

DIESEL LOCOMOTIVES

101 CLASS (DL)   Bo-Bo

Built: 1970 by BREL, Doncaster, as sub contractors for The Hunslet Engine Company.
Engine: English Electric 8CSVT of 1007 kW (1350 hp) at 850 rpm.
Transmission: Electric. English Electric 253AZ traction motors.
Weight: 69 tonnes.
Length: 13.77 m (45 ft 2 in).
Maximum Speed: 128 km/h (80 mph).

101	Eagle	103 (Z)	Merlin
102 (Z)	Falcon		

104 CLASS (MV)   Bo-Bo

Built: 1956-7 by MV. Rebuilt 1971-79 by Coras Iompair Éireann at Inchicore.
Engine: General Motors 8-B645E of 821 kW (1100 hp) at 900 rpm.
Transmission: Electric. MV MV137CW traction motors.
Weight: 61.5 tonnes.
Length: 12.80 m (42 ft).
Maximum Speed: 128 km/h (80 mph).
Note: Formerly CIE 216, 218, 227, 228, 230 & 234 respectively. 105 remained
to be converted at the time of going to press.

| 104 (Z) | 105 | 106 | 107 (Z) | 108 | 109 (Z) |

111 CLASS (GM)   Co-Co

Built: 1980-84 by General Motors.
Engine: General Motors 12-645E3B of 1845 kW (2475 hp) at 900 rpm.
Transmission: Electric. General Motors D77B traction motors.
Weight: 100.6 tonnes.
Length: 17.37 m (57 ft).
Maximum Speed: 143 km/h (89 mph).

| 111 | Great Northern | 113 | Belfast & Co Down |
| 112 | Northern Counties | | |

REPUBLIC OF IRELAND

Iarnród Éireann (IR)

Gauge: 1600 mm (5 ft 3 in).
Route Length: 1947 km.

Depot & Works

Inchicore (Located 2.8 km west of Dublin Heuston on the south side of the line).

Other Depots & Stabling Points

Cork, Dublin Connolly, Limerick.

Locomotives and rolling stock are also stabled at branch terminal staions over-night.

Railrover Information

8 Day IR Rambler Ticket: Unlimited standard class travel on IR services for any 8 days within a 15 day period. Prices: Ir£52 Adult, Ir£26 Child (3-15).
15 Day IR Rambler Ticket: Unlimited standard class travel on IR services for any 15 days within a 30 day period. Prices: Ir£77 Adult, Ir£38 Child (3-15).
8 Day Irish Rover Ticket: Issued in conjunction with Northern Ireland Railways. 8 days unlimited standard class travel on both IR & NIR services within a fixed 15 day period. Prices: Ir£65 Adult, Ir£32.50 Child (3-15).
DART One Day Rover: Unlimited standard class travel in the Dublin Sub-urban area bounded by Balbriggan, Kilcoole, Howth and Maynooth. Prices: Ir£2.50 Adult, Ir£1.25 Child (3-15). Available from stations within the area only.
Tickets & Details: CIE Tours International, Ireland House, New Bond Street, London. Also available at principal stations of IR. 8 Day Irish Rover Ticket is also available from NIR (qv).

DIESEL LOCOMOTIVES

001 CLASS (A)   Co-Co

Built: 1955-56 by MV. Rebuilt 1968-71 by Coras Iompair Éireann at Inchicore.
Engine: General Motors 12-645E of 989 kW (1325 hp) at 800 rpm. (* 12-645E of 1231 kW (1650 hp) at 900 rpm).
Transmission: Electric. MV MV137CW traction motors.
Weight: 83.3 tonnes.
Length: 15.545 m (51 ft).
Maximum Speed: 121 km/h (75 mph). [*128 km/h (80 mph)].

001	013	021	030	040 (Z)	052
002	014	022	031	042	053
003	015	023	033	043 (Z)	054*
005	016	025	035	047	055
007	017	026	036*	048	056*
009	018	027*	038	049	057
011	019	029 (Z)	039	051	058
012	020				

Top: IR 001 class no. 007 stands at Connolly depot still sporting CIE emblems.
(D. W. Fickes)

Bottom: IR 141 class no. 176 at Inchicore depot. *(D. W. Fickes)*

071 CLASS   Co-Co

Built: 1976 by General Motors.
Engine: General Motors 12-645E3B of 1845 kW (2475 hp) at 900 rpm.
Transmission: Electric. General Motors D77B traction motors.
Weight: 100.6 tonnes.
Length: 17.37 m (57 ft).
Maximum Speed: 143 km/h (89 mph).

071	~~074~~	~~077~~	080	083	086
072	~~075~~	078	~~081~~	084	087
~~073~~	076	~~079~~	~~082~~	085	088

121 CLASS (B)   Bo-Bo

Built: 1960 by General Motors.
Engine: General Motors 8-567CR of 709 kW (950 hp) at 835 rpm. (* 8-B645E of 821 kW (1100 hp) at 900 rpm).
Transmission: Electric. General Motors D47 traction motors.
Weight: 65 tonnes.
Length: 12.14 m (39 ft 10 in).
Maximum Speed: 124 km/h (77 mph).

121	124	127*	130	132	134
122	125 (Z)	~~128*~~	131	133	135
123	126*	129*			

141 CLASS (B)   Bo-Bo

Built: 1962 by General Motors.
Engine: General Motors 8-567CR of 709 kW (950 hp) at 835 rpm. (* 8-B645E of 821 kW (1100 hp) at 900 rpm).
Transmission: Electric. General Motors D57 traction motors.
Weight: 68 tonnes.   **Length:** 13.42 m (44 ft).
Maximum Speed: 124 km/h (77 mph).

~~141~~	148	~~154*~~	~~160~~	166	172
142	149	155	161	167*	~~173~~
143	150	156	~~162~~	168	174
144	~~151~~	157*	163*	~~169~~	175*
145*	152	158	164	170*	176
146	153	159	165	171	~~177~~
147					

202 208 209 221 223 231

Built: 1966 by General Motors.
Engine: General Motors 8-645E of 821 kW (1100 hp) at 900 rpm.
Transmission: Electric. General Motors D77 traction motors.
Weight: 68 tonnes.
Length: 13.42 m (44 ft).
Maximum Speed: 128 km/h (80 mph).

181	~~183~~	~~185~~	187	189	191
182	184	186	188	190	192

LUXEMBOURG

Societé National des Chemins de Fer Luxembourgeois (CFL).

Gauge: 1435 mm (4 ft 8½ in).
Route Length: 270 km.

Depot & Works

Luxembourg.

Other Depots & Stabling Points

Bettembourg Yard, Esch sur Alzette, Pétange, Wasserbillig. Locomtoives may also stable at branch terminal stations, particularly overnight.

Railrover Information

Benelux-Tourrail: 5 days unlimited travel on all SNCB/NMBS, NS & CFL services within a predetermined 17 day period. Prices: Adult (above 25) 2nd Class £43.50, 1st Class £65.00. Junior (4-25 years) £31.00 2nd Class, £46.00 1st Class. Passport number details required. Juniors will be required to have proof of age before tickets can be issued.
Network Ticket: One day unlimited 2nd Class travel on all CFL trains and buses. Not valid from ticket-frontier points with neighbouring countries. Price: 217 Luxembourg Francs.

5-Day Network Ticket: 5 days unlimited 2nd Class travel on all CFL trains and buses within a 31 day period. Not valid to or from ticket-frontier points with neighbouring countries. Price: 658 Luxembourg Francs.

One Month Network Ticket: One month unlimited 2nd Class travel on all CFL trains and buses. Available only for calendar months. Not valid to or from ticket-frontier points with neighbouring countries. Price: 1748 Luxembourg Francs.

Tickets & Details: Benelux-Tourrail tickets are available from Netherlands Railways (qv). The Network tickets are available from all rail stations within Luxembourg only. Other information is available from : Luxembourg National Trade & Tourist Office, 36-37 Piccadilly, London, W1V 9PA. (Telephone 01-434-2800).

DIESEL LOCOMOTIVES

800 CLASS   Bo-Bo

Built: 1954 by AFB.
Engine: General Motors 8-567B of 650 kW (875 hp) at 835 rpm.
Transmission: Electric. General Motors traction motors.
Weight: 74 tonnes.
Length: 13.80 m (45 ft 3 in).
Maximum Speed: 80 km/h (50 mph).

801	802	803	804	805	806

850 CLASS   Bo-Bo

Built: 1956-57 by B & L.
Engine: SACM MGO V12SH of 615 kW (825 hp).
Transmission: Electric. B & L traction motors.
Weight: 72 tonnes.
Length: 14.75 m (48 ft 5 in).
Maximum Speed: 105 km/h (65 mph).

851	853	855	856	857	858
852	854				

Top: CFL 900 class no 901 at Luxembourg on 25.03.89.   (D. J. Glossop)

Bottom: CFL 1020 class no. 1021 at Luxembourg Depot on 25.02.89.   (D. Rowland)

900 CLASS   Bo-Bo

Built: 1958 by B & L.
Engine: SACM MGO V12SHR of 690 kW (925 hp).
Transmission: Electric. B & L traction motors.
Weight: 72 tonnes.   **Length:** 14.75 m (48 ft 5 in).
Maximum Speed: 105 km/h (65 mph).

901					
902	Steinfurt				
903	905	907	909	911	913
904	906	908	910	912	

1000 CLASS   B

Built: 1972 by Jung.
Engine: Deutz F12 L413 of 186 kW (240 hp).
Transmission: Hydraulic. Voith.
Weight: 32 tonnes.   **Length:** 7.20 m (23 ft 7 in).
Maximum Speed: 60 km/h (37 mph).

1001	1002	1003	1004

1010 CLASS   B

Built: 1964 by Henschel.
Engine: Henschel 6R 1215A of 160 kW (210 hp).
Transmission: Hydraulic. Voith.
Length: 7.10 m (23 ft 4 in).
Maximum Speed: 24 km/h (15 mph).

1010

1020 CLASS   B

Built: 1952-57 by Deutz.
Engine: Deutz A8 L614 of 100 kW (134 hp).
Transmission: Hydraulic. Voith.
Weight: 22 tonnes.
Length: 7.57 m (24 ft 10 in).
Maximum Speed: 53 km/h (33 mph).

1021	1022	1023	1024

Top: CFL 1800 class no. 1819 at Liege Guillemans with train IR121, 1912 Liege-Luxembourg on 16.07.89. *(R. G. Morris)*

Bottom: CFL 3600 class no. 3611 heads a line up of the class including 3618, 3609, 3604, 3619, 3608 & 3616 at Luxembourg Depot on 16.07.89. *(R. G. Morris)*

1030 CLASS   B

Built: 1988 by Jenbacher.
Engine: MTU 8V 183 TA12 of   kW (hp).
Transmission: Hydraulic. Voith L2r4SV2.
Weight: 36 tonnes.
Length: 8.55 m (28 ft 1 in).
Maximum Speed: 60 km/h (37 mph).

1031	1032	1033

1600 CLASS   Co-Co

Built: 1955 by AFB.
Engine: General Motors 16-567C of 1190 kW (1600 hp) at 835 rpm.
Transmission: Electric.
Weight: 108 tonnes.
Length: 19.01 m (62 ft 4 in).
Maximum Speed: 120 km/h (75 mph).

1602	1604 Fond-de-Gras
1603	

1800 CLASS   Co-Co

Built: 1963 by BN/ACEC/SEM.
Engine: General Motors 16-567C of 1340 kW (1800 hp) at 835 rpm.
Transmission: Electric.
Weight: 110 (*114) tonnes.
Length: 19.55 m (64 ft 2 in).
Maximum Speed: 120 km/h (75 mph).

1801*		1811	Ettelbruck
1802*	Blankenberge	1812	
1803*		1813	
1804*		1814	
1805	Mondorf-Les-Bains	1815*	Kautenbach 1881-1981
1806	Commune de Walferdange	1816*	Larochette
1807	Commune de Petange	1817*	
1808		1818*	
1809		1819*	Prince Henri
1810		1820*	Bettembourg

ELECTRIC LOCOMOTIVES

3600 CLASS   Bo-Bo

Built: 1958-59 by SEM.
Supply System: 25 kV ac overhead.
Traction Motors: MTE.
Continuous rating: 2680 kW (3600 hp).
Weight: 84 tonnes.
Length: 15.20 m (49 ft 10 in).
Maximum Speed: 120 km/h (75 mph).

3601		3611	
3602		3612	
3603		3613	Guillaume Luxembourg
3604		3614	Rumelange
3605		3616	Dudelange
3606	Dudelange	3617	
3607	Esch/Alzette	3618	Wiltz
3608		3619	Wasserbillig
3609		3620	Reiserbahn
3610			

BELGIUM

Société Nationale des Chemins de fer Belges (SNCB).
Nationale Maatschappij der Belgische Spoorwegen (NMBS).

Gauge: 1435 mm (4 ft 8< in).
Route Length: 3667 km.

Depots

Depots with a locomotive allocation, together with the official codes are:

FBMZ	Brussels Midi/Zuid
FCR	Charleroi Sud
FEO	Ronet (Namur)
FFO	Forest-Vorst
FGH	St. Ghislain
FGSP	Gent St. Pieters
FHS	Hasselt
FKR	Merelbeke (Gent)
FMS	Mons
FNDM	Antwerpen Dam
FNR	Namur
FSD	Oostende
FSR	Schaarbeek Diesel
FVY	Gouvy
FWO	Wondelgem
GMN	Montzen
GT	Haine St. Pierre
LBC	Bascoup
LK	Kortrijk
LNC	Monceau (Charleroi)
MGR	Angleur
MKM	Stockem (Arlon)
MUT	Latour
NK	Kinkempois (Liège)

Other Depots & Stabling Points

Aalst, Aarschot, Antwerpen Central, Antwerpen Noord, Antwerpen Oost, Antwerpen Schijnpoort, Arlon, Ath, Berchem, Bertrix, Brugge, Châtelet, De Panne, Denderleeuw, Dendermonde, Geraardsbergen, Huy, Jemelle, Leuven, Liers, Liège Guillemins, Mechelen, Mol, Ottignes, Oudenaarde, Schaarbeek Electric, Tournai, Turnhout, Virton, Visé, Welkenraedt.

Works

Mechelen - Electric Locomotives of classes 15, 16, 22, 23, 25.5 & 28, DMU & EMU.
Salzinnes - Diesel Locomotives & Electric Locomotives of classes 11, 12, 18, 20, 21, 26 & 27.

Railrover Information

Belgian-Tourrail: 5 days unlimited travel on all SNCB/NMBS services within a 17 day period. Prices (1989): Bfr 2550 Adult (26+) 1st Class, Bfr 1700 Adult (26+) 2nd class, Bfr 1950 Youth (12-25) 1st Class, Bfr 1300 Youth (12-25) 2nd Class. No Child fares available.
Belgian 16 day Runabout Ticket: 16 consecutive days unlimited travel on all SNCB/NMBS services. Prices (1989): Bfr 4580 1st Class, 3050 2nd Class. No reduced fares.
Benelux-Tourrail: 5 days unlimited travel on all SNCB/NMBS, NS & CFL services within a predetermined 17 day period. Prices : Adult (26+) 1st Class £65.00, 2nd Class £43.50. Junior (4-25 years) 1st Class £46.00, 2nd Class £31.00. Passport details required. Juniors will be required to show proof of age before tickets are issued.
Carte T.T.B.: 5 days unliimited travel on all SNCB/NMBS, SNCV (Belgian National Bus & Tram Company) & Société Intercommunales train, tram & bus services within a 17 day period. Prices (1989): Bfr 3050 Adult (26+) 1st Class, Bfr 2200 Adult (26+) 2nd Class, Bfr 2350 Young Person (under 26) 1st Class, Bfr 1700 Young Person (Under 26) 2nd Class.
Tickets & Details: Benelux-Tourrail tickets are available from Netherlands Railways (qv). All other tickets may be obtained via the Belgian National Tourist Office, 38 Dover Street, London, W1X 3RB. (Tel: 01 499 5379). All tickets are also available from SNCB/NMBS stations. Passport number details & specimen signature are required to purchase all tickets except the Carte T.T.B. We apologise for being unable to quote 1990 prices for the above tickets. This is due to the former Belgian Railways office in London having closed, leaving no forwarding address.

ELECTRIC LOCOMOTIVES

11 CLASS   Bo-Bo

Built: 1985-86 by BN.
Supply System: 3000/1500 V dc (dual voltage) overhead.
Traction Motors: ACEC LE622S frame mounted.
Continuous rating: 3125 kW (4180 hp).
Weight: 84 tonnes.
Length: 18.65 m (61 ft 2 in).
Maximum Speed: 160 km/h (100 mph).

1181 FBMZ	1185 FBMZ	1189 FBMZ
1182 FBMZ	1186 FBMZ	1190 FBMZ
1183 FBMZ	1187 FBMZ	1191 FBMZ
1184 FBMZ	1188 FBMZ	1192 FBMZ

12 CLASS   Bo-Bo

Built: 1986 by BN.
Supply System: 3000 V dc/25 kV ac (dual voltage) overhead.
Traction Motors: ACEC LE622S frame mounted.
Continuous rating: 3125 kW (4180 hp).
Weight: 84 tonnes.
Length: 18.65 m (61 ft 2 in).
Maximum Speed: 160 km/h (100 mph).

1201 FBMZ	1205 FBMZ	1209 FBMZ
1202 FBMZ	1206 FBMZ	1210 FBMZ
1203 FBMZ	1207 FBMZ	1211 FBMZ
1204 FBMZ	1208 FBMZ	1212 FBMZ

15 CLASS   Bo-Bo

Built: 1962 by BN.
Supply System: 3000 V dc/1500 V dc/25 kV ac (triple voltage) overhead.
Traction Motors: ACEC ES541 frame mounted.
Continuous rating: 2620 kW (3505 hp).
Weight: 77.7 tonnes.
Length: 17.75 m (58 ft 3 in).
Maximum Speed: 160 km/h (100 mph).

Top: SNCB 11 class no. 1185 double headed with preserved BR EM2 class no. E27000 "ELECTRA" at Westhaven during a railtour duty on 29.07.89.
(D. J. Glossop)

Bottom: SNCB 18 class no. 1801 arrives at Liege Guillemans during March 1980.
(P. R. Marsh)

1501 FBMZ	1503 FBMZ	1505 FBMZ
1502 FBMZ	1504 FBMZ	

16 CLASS   Bo-Bo

Built: 1966 by BN.
Supply System: 3000 V dc/1500 V dc/25 kV ac/15 kV ac (quadruple voltage) overhead.
Traction Motors: ACEC ES541 frame mounted.
Continuous rating: 2620 kW (3505 hp).
Weight: 82.6 tonnes.
Length: 16.65 m (54 ft 8 in).
Maximum Speed: 160 km/h (100 mph).

1601 FBMZ	1604 FBMZ	1607 FBMZ
1602 FBMZ	1605 FBMZ	1608 FBMZ
1603 FBMZ	1606 FBMZ	

18 CLASS   C-C

Built: 1973-74 by BN.
Supply System: 3000 V dc/1500 V dc/25 kV ac/15 kV ac (quadruple voltage) overhead.
Traction Motors: 2 Alsthom TDQ662C1 frame mounted.
Continuous rating: 4320 kW (5780 hp).
Weight: 113 tonnes.
Length: 22.08 m (72 ft 5 in).
Maximum Speed: 180 km/h (112 mph).

1801 NK	1803 NK	1805 NK
1802 NK	1804 NK	1806 NK

20 CLASS   Co-Co

Built: 1975-78 by BN.
Supply System: 3000 V dc overhead.
Traction Motors: ACEC LE772G frame mounted.
Continuous rating: 5130 kW (6865 hp).
Weight: 110 tonnes.
Length: 19.50 m (64 ft).
Maximum Speed: 160 km/h (100 mph).

Top: SNCB 23 class no. 2330 arrives at Liege Guillemans with a NATO troop special in March 1980. *(P. R. Marsh)*

Bottom: SNCB 26 class no. 2622 at Liege Guillemans with a local working. *(P. R. Marsh)*

2001 FEO	2010 FEO	2018 FEO
2002 FEO	2011 FEO	2019 FEO
2003 FEO	2012 FEO	2020 FEO
2004 FEO	2013 FEO	2021 FEO
2005 FEO	2014 FEO	2022 FEO
2006 FEO	2015 FEO	2023 FEO
2007 FEO	2016 FEO	2024 FEO
2008 FEO	2017 FEO	2025 FEO
2009 FEO		

21 CLASS   Bo-Bo

Built: 1984-88 by BN.
Supply System: 3000 V dc overhead.
Traction Motors: ACEC LE622S frame mounted.
Continuous rating: 3140 kW (4200 hp).
Weight: 84 tonnes.
Length: 18.65 m (61 ft 2 in).
Maximum Speed: 160 km/h (100 mph).

2101 FKR	2121 FKR	2141 FKR
2102 FKR	2122 FKR	2142 FKR
2103 FKR	2123 FKR	2143 FKR
2104 FKR	2124 FKR	2144 FKR
2105 FKR	2125 FKR	2145 FKR
2106 FKR	2126 FKR	2146 FKR
2107 FKR	2127 FKR	2147 FKR
2108 FKR	2128 FKR	2148 FKR
2109 FKR	2129 FKR	2149 FKR
2110 FKR	2130 FKR	2150 FKR
2111 FKR	2131 FKR	2151 FKR
2112 FKR	2132 FKR	2152 FKR
2113 FKR	2133 FKR	2153 FKR
2114 FKR	2134 FKR	2154 FKR
2115 FKR	2135 FKR	2155 FKR
2116 FKR	2136 FKR	2156 FKR
2117 FKR	2137 FKR	2157 FKR
2118 FKR	2138 FKR	2158 FKR
2119 FKR	2139 FKR	2159 FKR
2120 FKR	2140 FKR	2160 FKR

22 CLASS   Bo-Bo

Built: 1954 by BN.
Supply System: 3000 V dc overhead.
Traction Motors: ACEC/SEMG CF729.
Continuous rating: 1740 kW (2330 hp).
Weight: 87 tonnes.
Length: 18.00 m (59 ft 1 in).
Maximum Speed: 130 km/h (81 mph).

2201 FGH	2218 FGH	2235 FGH
2202 FGH	2219 FGH	2236 FGH
2203 FGH	2220 FGH	2237 FGH
2204 FGH	2221 FGH	2238 FGH
2205 FGH	2222 FGH	2239 FGH
2206 FGH	2223 FGH	2240 FGH
2207 FGH	2224 FGH	2241 FGH
2208 FGH	2225 FGH	2242 FGH
2209 FGH	2226 FGH	2243 FGH
2210 FGH	2227 FGH	2244 FGH
2211 FGH	2228 FGH	2245 FGH
2212 FGH	2229 FGH	2246 FGH
2213 FGH	2230 FGH	2247 FGH
2214 FGH	2231 FGH	2248 FGH
2215 FGH	2232 FGH	2249 FGH
2216 FGH	2233 FGH	2250 FGH
2217 FGH	2234 FGH	

23 CLASS   Bo-Bo

Built: 1955-7 by Niv.
Supply System: 3000 V dc overhead.
Traction Motors: ACEC/SEMG CF729.
Continuous rating: 1740 kW (2330 hp).
Weight: 93.3 tonnes.
Length: 18.00 m (59 ft 1 in).
Maximum Speed: 130 km/h (81 mph).

2301 FEO	2306 FEO	2311 FEO
2302 FEO	2307 FEO	2312 FEO
2303 FEO	2308 FEO	2313 FEO
2304 FEO	2309 FEO	2314 FEO
2305 FEO	2310 FEO	2315 FEO

2316 FEO	2339 FEO	2362 FEO
2317 FEO	2340 FEO	2363 FEO
2318 FEO	2341 FEO	2364 NK
2319 FEO	2342 FEO	2365 NK
2320 FEO	2343 FEO	2366 NK
2321 FEO	2344 FEO	2367 NK
2322 FEO	2345 FEO	2368 NK
2323 FEO	2346 FEO	2369 NK
2324 FEO	2347 FEO	2370 NK
2325 FEO	2348 FEO	2371 NK
2326 FEO	2349 FEO	2372 NK
2327 FEO	2350 FEO	2373 NK
2328 FEO	2351 FEO	2374 NK
2329 FEO	2352 FEO	2375 NK
2330 FEO	2353 FEO	2376 NK
2331 FEO	2354 FEO	2377 NK
2332 FEO	2355 FEO	2378 NK
2333 FEO	2356 FEO	2379 NK
2334 FEO	2357 FEO	2380 NK
2335 FEO	2358 FEO	2381 NK
2336 FEO	2359 FEO	2382 NK
2337 FEO	2360 FEO	2383 NK
2338 FEO	2361 FEO	

25 CLASS   Bo-Bo

Built: 1960 by BN.
Supply System: 3000 V dc overhead.
Traction Motors: ACEC/SEMG CF729.
Continuous rating: 1740 kW (2330 hp).
Weight: 83.9 tonnes.
Length: 18.00 m (59 ft 1 in).
Maximum Speed: 130 km/h (81 mph).

2501 FBMZ	2506 FBMZ	2511 FBMZ
2502 FBMZ	2507 FBMZ	2512 FBMZ
2503 FBMZ	2508 FBMZ	2513 FBMZ
2504 FBMZ	2509 FBMZ	2514 FBMZ
2505 FBMZ	2510 FBMZ	

Top: SNCB 27 class no. 2747 runs light through Liege Guillemans on 14.07.89.
(D. W. Fickes)

Bottom: SNCB diesels 5312+5502 double-head a freight working bound for Ronet Yard through Namur on 18.10.88. *(R. G. Morris)*

25.5 CLASS   Bo-Bo

Built: 1960 by BN. Modified to dual voltage 1973.
Supply System: 3000/1500 V dc overhead (dual voltage).
Traction Motors: ACEC/SEMG CF729.
Continuous rating: 1740 kW (2330 hp).
Weight: 85 tonnes.
Length: 18.00 m (59 ft 1 in).
Maximum Speed: 130 km/h (81 mph).

2551 FBMZ	2554 FBMZ	2557 FBMZ
2552 FBMZ	2555 FBMZ	2558 FBMZ
2553 FBMZ	2556 FBMZ	

26 CLASS   B-B

Built: 1964/69-72 by BN.
Supply System: 3000 V dc overhead.
Traction Motors: 2 ACEC 2ES508 frame mounted.
Continuous rating: 2240 kW (2995 hp)[2601-5]; 2470 kW (3305 hp)
[others].
Weight: 82.4 tonnes.
Length: 17.28 m (56 ft 5 in).
Maximum Speed: 130 km/h (81 mph).

2601 MKM	2613 MKM	2625 MKM
2602 MKM	2614 MKM	2626 MKM
2603 MKM	2615 MKM	2627 MKM
2604 MKM	2616 MKM	2628 MKM
2605 MKM	2617 MKM	2629 MKM
2606 MKM	2618 MKM	2630 MKM
2607 MKM	2619 MKM	2631 MKM
2608 MKM	2620 MKM	2632 MKM
2609 MKM	2621 MKM	2633 MKM
2610 MKM	2622 MKM	2634 MKM
2611 MKM	2623 MKM	2635 MKM
2612 MKM	2624 MKM	

27 CLASS   Bo-Bo

Built: 1981-84 by BN.
Supply System: 3000 V dc overhead.
Traction Motors: ACEC LE921S frame mounted.
Continuous rating: 4150 kW (5550 hp).
Weight: 85 tonnes.
Length: 18.65 m (61 ft 2 in).
Maximum Speed: 160 km/h (100 mph).

2701 FSD	2721 NK	2741 NK
2702 FSD	2722 NK	2742 NK
2703 FSD	2723 NK	2743 NK
2704 FSD	2724 NK	2744 NK
2705 FSD	2725 NK	2745 NK
2706 FSD	2726 NK	2746 NK
2707 FSD	2727 NK	2747 NK
2708 FSD	2728 NK	2748 NK
2709 FSD	2729 NK	2749 NK
2710 FSD	2730 NK	2750 NK
2711 FSD	2731 NK	2751 NK
2712 FSD	2732 NK	2752 NK
2713 FSD	2733 NK	2753 NK
2714 FSD	2734 NK	2754 NK
2715 FSD	2735 NK	2755 NK
2716 FSD	2736 NK	2756 NK
2717 FSD	2737 NK	2757 NK
2718 FSD	2738 NK	2758 NK
2719 FSD	2739 NK	2759 NK
2720 FSD	2740 NK	2760 NK

28 CLASS   Bo-Bo

Built: 1949 by BM.
Supply System: 3000 V dc overhead.
Traction Motors: ACEC/SEMG CF729.
Continuous rating: 1620 kW (2170 hp).
Weight: 85 tonnes.
Length: 17.18 m (56 ft 5 in).
Maximum Speed: 130 km/h (81 mph).

2801 FBMZ	2802 FBMZ	2803 FBMZ

DIESEL LOCOMOTIVES

51 CLASS   Co-Co

Built: 1961 by Cockerill.
Engine: Cockerill 10-608A of 1457 kW (1950 hp) at 650 rpm.
Transmission: Electric. ACEC/SEM traction motors.
Weight: 117 tonnes.
Length: 20.16 m (66 ft 2 in).
Maximum Speed: 120 km/h (75 mph).

5101 FSR	5130 FHS	5159 FNDM
5102 FSR	5131 LNC	5160 FNDM
5103 FSR	5132 FKR	5162 FNDM
5104 FSR	5133 FHS	5163 FNDM
5105 FSR	5134 FKR	5164 FNDM
5106 FSR	5135 LNC	5166 FNDM
5107 FKR	5136 FHS	5167 FNDM
5108 FKR	5137 FHS	5168 FNDM
5109 FKR	5138 FHS	5170 FNDM
5110 FKR	5139 LNC	5171 FNDM
5111 FKR	5140 LNC	5172 FNDM
5112 FKR	5141 LNC	5173 FNDM
5113 FKR	5142 FHS	5174 FNDM
5114 FSR	5143 FHS	5175 FNDM
5115 FKR	5144 FHS	5177 FNDM
5116 FKR	5145 FHS	5178 FNDM
5117 LNC	5146 LNC	5179 FHS
5118 FKR	5147 LNC	5180 FNDM
5119 FKR	5148 LNC	5181 FNDM
5120 LNC	5149 LNC	5182 FNDM
5121 LNC	5150 LNC	5183 FNDM
5122 FSR	5151 FHS	5184 FNDM
5123 LNC	5152 FHS	5185 FHS
5124 FKR	5153 FHS	5186 FNDM
5125 FKR	5154 FNDM	5187 FHS
5126 LNC	5155 FNDM	5189 FNDM
5127 FHS	5156 FNDM	5192 FHS
5128 FKR	5157 FNDM	5193 FHS
5129 FHS	5158 FNDM	

Top: SNCB 55 class no. 5508 at Gouvy on 16.07.89. *(D. W. Fickes)*

Bottom: SNCB 59 class no. 5946 at Raeren with a railtour working on 12.08.89. *(D. J. Glossop)*

52 CLASS   Co-Co

Built: 1955 by AFB.
Engine: General Motors 16-567C of 1285 kW (1720 hp) at 835 rpm.
Transmission: Electric. General Motors traction motors.
Weight: 108 tonnes.
Length: 18.85 m (61 ft 10 in).
Maximum Speed: 120 km/h (75 mph).

5201 FEO	5211 FEO	5215 FEO
5202 FEO	5212 FEO	5216 FEO
5205 FEO	5213 FEO	5217 MUT
5209 MUT	5214 FEO	

53 CLASS   Co-Co

Built: 1955 by AFB.
Engine: General Motors 16-567C of 1285 kW (1720 hp) at 835 rpm.
Transmission: Electric. General Motors traction motors.
Weight: 106.6 tonnes.
Length: 18.85 m (61 ft 10 in).
Maximum Speed: 120 km/h (75 mph).

5301 MUT	5308 MUT	5315 MUT
5302 FEO	5309 MUT	5316 MUT
5303 MUT	5310 MUT	5317 FEO
5304 MUT	5311 MUT	5318 FEO
5305 MUT	5312 MUT	5319 MUT
5306 MUT	5313 MUT	5320 FEO
5307 FEO	5314 MUT	

54 CLASS   Co-Co

Built: 1957 by AFB.
Engine: General Motors 16-567C of 1285 kW (1720 hp) at 835 rpm.
Transmission: Electric. General Motors traction motors.
Weight: 108 tonnes.   **Length:** 18.85 m (61 ft 10 in).
Maximum Speed: 120 km/h (75 mph).

5401 FEO	5404 FEO	5407 FEO
5403 FEO		

55 CLASS   Co-Co

Built: 1961 by BN.
Engine: General Motors 16-567C of 1457 kW (1950 hp) at 835 rpm.
Transmission: Electric. ACEC/SEM traction motors.
Weight: 110 tonnes.
Length: 19.55 m (64 ft 2 in).
Maximum Speed: 120 km/h (75 mph).

5501 MUT	5515 NK	5530 NK
5502 MUT	5517 NK	5531 NK
5503 MUT	5518 NK	5532 NK
5504 MUT	5519 NK	5533 NK
5505 NK	5520 NK	5534 NK
5506 NK	5521 NK	5535 NK
5507 NK	5523 NK	5536 NK
5508 NK	5524 NK	5537 NK
5509 NK	5525 NK	5538 NK
5510 NK	5526 NK	5539 NK
5511 NK	5527 NK	5540 NK
5512 NK	5528 NK	5541 NK
5513 NK	5529 NK	5542 NK
5514 NK		

59 CLASS   Bo-Bo

Built: 1955 by Cockerill/BM.
Engine: Cockerill/Baldwin 608A of 1308 kW (1750 hp) at 625 rpm.
Transmission: Electric. ACEC/Westinghouse traction motors.
Weight: 87.2 tonnes.
Length: 16.18 m (53 ft 1 in).
Maximum Speed: 120 km/h (75 mph).

5905 FNDM(Z)	5910 FNDM	5936 FNDM(Z)
5909 FNDM(Z)	5926 FNDM(Z)	5946 FNDM(Z)

YOUR PHOTOGRAPHS WANTED NOW - See
page 18 !

60 CLASS   Bo-Bo

Built: 1961 by Cockerill.
Engine: Cockerill/Baldwin TH895SA of 1046 kW (1400 hp) at 1000 rpm.
Transmission: Electric. ACEC traction motors.
Weight: 85.4 tonnes.
Length: 17.35 m (56 ft 11 in).
Maximum Speed: 120 km/h (75 mph).

6016 FKR	6073 FKR	6089 FGH
6042 FGH	6086 FKR	

SNCB 16 class no. 1603 on DB metals with a Köln service at Aachen Hbf.
(P. R. Marsh)

62 CLASS   Bo-Bo

Built: 1961-66 by BN.
Engine: General Motors 12-567C of 1065 kW (1425 hp) at 835 rpm.
Transmission: Electric. ACEC/GM traction motors.
Weight: 80-81.6 tonnes.
Length: 16.79 m (55 ft 1 in).
Maximum Speed: 120 km/h (75 mph).

Top: SNCB 60 class no. 6029 at Gouvy Depot on 16.07.89. *(D. W. Fickes)*

Bottom: SNCB 62 class no. 6295 heads a line up of the class at Hasselt Depot on 15.07.89. *(D. W. Fickes)*

6201 FKR	6248 LNC	6292 FKR
6202 FKR	6249 LNC	6293 FKR
6203 FKR	6250 FGH	6294 FHS
6204 FKR	6251 FHS	6295 FHS
6205 FKR	6252 FHS	6296 FHS(Z)
6206 FKR	6253 FHS	6297 FHS
6207 FKR	6254 FGH	6298 FHS
6210 FKR	6255 FHS	6299 FHS(Z)
6211 FKR	6256 FKR	6300 LK
6212 FKR	6257 FGH(Z)	6301 LK
6213 FKR	6258 FGH	6302 LK
6214 FKR	6260 FHS	6303 LK
6215 LK	6261 FHS	6304 LK
6216 FKR	6262 FGH	6305 LK
6217 LNC	6263 FGH	6306 LK
6218 LNC	6264 FHS	6307 LK
6219 FKR	6265 FKR	6309 FKR
6220 FKR	6266 FGH	6311 FKR
6221 FKR	6267 FHS	6312 FKR
6222 FKR	6268 FHS	6313 FKR
6223 FKR	6269 FGH	6314 FGH
6224 LNC	6270 FGH	6315 FKR
6225 FKR	6271 LNC	6316 FHS
6227 FKR	6272 FGH	6317 FHS
6228 FKR	6273 FGH	6318 FHS
6229 FKR	6274 NK	6319 FHS
6230 FKR	6275 FGH	6320 FGH
6231 LNC	6276 FGH	6321 FHS
6233 FKR	6277 FGH	6322 FKR
6234 LNC	6278 FGH	6323 NK
6235 FKR	6279 FHS	6324 NK
6236 FKR	6281 FHS	6325 NK
6237 FKR	6282 FGH	6326 FHS
6238 FHS	6283 FHS	6327 FHS(Z)
6240 FHS	6284 FGH	6328 NK
6241 FGH(Z)	6285 FGH	6329 NK
6242 FGH(Z)	6286 FGH	6330 FHS
6243 LNC	6287 FGH	6331 FHS
6244 FGH	6288 FGH	6333 FKR
6245 FHS	6289 NK	6391 FKR
6246 FHS	6290 FGH	6392 FKR
6247 FKR	6291 FHS	6393 FKR

37

70 CLASS

Bo-Bo

Built: 1954 by BM.
Engine: ABC 8DUS of 523 kW (700 hp) at 750 rpm.
Transmission: Electric. ACEC/Westinghouse traction motors.
Weight: 83 tonnes.
Length: 12.15 m (39 ft 10 in).
Maximum Speed: 50 km/h (31 mph).

7001 FNDM	7003 FNDM	7005 FNDM
7002 FNDM	7004 FNDM	7006 FNDM

71 CLASS

B-B

Built: 1962 by ABR. Rebuilt 1980 at SNCB Salzinnes Works.
Engine: ABC 6XDC 100-750A of 523 kW (700 hp) at 750 rpm.
Transmission: Hydraulic. Voith L217 torque converter.
Weight: 74 tonnes.
Length: 13.35 m (43 ft 10 in).
Maximum Speed: 80 km/h (50 mph).

7101 FNDM	7102 FNDM	7103 FNDM

73 CLASS

C

Built: 1965-77 by BN & ABR.
Engine: Cockerill 6TH695SA or 6T240CO of 560 kW (750 hp) at 950 rpm.
Transmission: Hydraulic. Voith L217U torque converter.
Weight: 56 tonnes.
Length: 11.17 m (36 ft 8 in).
Maximum Speed: 60 km/h (37 mph).

7301 LNC	7310 LNC	7319 LNC
7302 LNC	7311 LNC	7320 LNC
7303 LNC	7312 LNC	7321 LNC
7304 LNC	7313 LNC	7322 LNC
7305 LNC	7314 LNC	7323 LNC
7306 LNC	7315 LNC	7324 LNC
7307 LNC	7316 LNC	7325 LNC
7308 LNC	7317 LNC	7326 LNC
7309 LNC	7318 LNC	7327 LNC

7328 LNC	7351 FKR	7374 FHS
7329 LNC	7352 FKR	7375 FHS
7330 LNC	7353 FKR	7376 FKR
7331 LNC	7354 FKR	7377 FKR
7332 LNC	7355 FKR	7378 FKR
7333 LNC	7356 FKR	7379 FKR
7334 LNC	7357 FHS	7380 FKR
7335 LNC	7358 FKR	7381 NK
7336 FHS	7359 FKR	7382 NK
7337 FKR	7360 FKR	7383 NK
7338 FEO	7361 FKR	7384 NK
7339 FEO	7362 FKR	7385 NK
7340 FEO	7363 FKR	7386 NK
7341 FEO	7364 FKR	7387 FHS
7342 FEO	7365 FHS	7388 NK
7343 NK	7366 FHS	7389 NK
7344 NK	7367 FKR	7390 NK
7345 NK	7368 FKR	7391 NK
7346 NK	7369 FKR	7392 FHS
7347 NK	7370 FKR	7393 FHS
7348 NK	7371 FHS	7394 FHS
7349 NK	7372 FKR	7395 FHS
7350 FKR	7373 FHS	

74 CLASS   C

Built: 1977 by BN.
Engine: ABC 6DXS 560 kW (750 hp) at 750 rpm.
Transmission: Hydraulic. Voith L217U torque converter.
Weight: 59 tonnes.
Length: 11.17 m (36 ft 8 in).
Maximum   Speed: 60 km/h (37 mph).

7401 FNDM	7405 FNDM	7408 FNDM
7402 FNDM	7406 FNDM	7409 FNDM
7403 FNDM	7407 FNDM	7410 FNDM
7404 FNDM		

Top: SNCB 71 class no. 7102 at Antwerpen Dam Depot on 03.12.89. (D. Rowland)

Bottom: SNCB 82 class no. 8247 passes Berchem with the ecs for a P train from Antwerpen Central on 23.03.89. (D. J. Glossop)

75 CLASS   B-B

Built: 1965 by BN.
Engine: General Motors 12-657D-1 (two stroke) of 1090 kW (1460 hp) at 835 rpm.
Transmission: Hydraulic. Voith L216 torque converter.
Weight: 79 tonnes.   **Length:** 16.79 m (55 ft 1 in).
Maximum Speed: 120 km/h (75 mph).

7501 FNDM	7503 FNDM	7505 FNDM
7502 FNDM	7504 FNDM	7506 FNDM

80 CLASS   C

Built: 1960-63 by BN & ABR.
Engine: Maybach GT06A of 485 kW (650 hp) at 1400 rpm.
Transmission: Hydraulic. Voith L37 torque converter.
Weight: 52.1 tonnes.   **Length:** 10.36 m (34 ft).
Maximum Speed: 78 km/h (49 mph).

8001 FSR	8032 FSR	8053 FKR
8002 FSR	8033 FSR	8055 FSR
8006 FSR	8034 FSR	8058 FSR
8007 FSR	8035 FSR	8059 FSR
8008 FSR	8037 FSR	8061 FSR
8009 FSR	8040 FSR	8062 FSR
8011 FSR	8045 FSR	8063 FSR
8012 FSR	8046 FSR	8064 FSR
8018 FSR	8047 FSR	8065 FSR
8020 FSR	8049 FSR	8066 FSR
8025 FSR	8050 FSR	8067 FSR
8027 FSR	8051 FSR	8068 FSR
8031 FSR	8052 FSR	8069 FSR

82 CLASS   C

Built: 1965-73 by BN & ABR.
Engine: ABC 6DXS of 485 kW (650 hp) at 750 rpm.
Transmission: Hydraulic. Voith L217U torque converter.
Weight: 56-59 tonnes.
Length: 11.17 m or 11.32 m (36 ft 8 in or 37 ft 2 in).
Maximum Speed: 60 km/h (37 mph).

8201 FSD	8226 NK	8251 FGH
8202 FSD	8227 FGH	8252 NK
8203 FVY	8228 FGH	8253 NK
8204 FSD	8229 FGH	8254 FGH
8205 NK	8230 FGH	8255 NK
8206 FSD	8231 FGH	8256 FNDM
8207 FSD	8232 FNDM	8257 FNDM
8208 FSD	8233 FSD	8258 NK
8209 FSD	8234 NK	8259 FNDM
8210 FSD	8235 NK	8260 FNDM
8211 FSD	8236 FNDM	8261 FNDM
8212 FGH	8237 NK	8262 FNDM
8213 NK	8238 NK	8263 FNDM
8214 FGH	8239 NK	8264 FNDM
8215 NK	8240 NK	8265 FNDM
8216 NK	8241 FGH	8266 FNDM
8217 FGH	8242 FSD	8267 FNDM
8218 FGH	8243 FSD	8268 FNDM
8219 FGH	8244 FSD	8269 FNDM
8220 FVY	8245 NK	8270 FNDM
8221 FGH	8246 FNDM	8271 FNDM
8222 FGH	8247 FNDM	8272 FNDM
8223 FGH	8248 NK	8273 FNDM
8224 NK	8249 FSD	8274 FNDM
8225 NK	8250 FSD	8275 FNDM

83 CLASS   C

Built: 1956 by Cockerill.
Engine: Cockerill/Hamilton 695SA of 410 kW (550 hp) at 450 rpm.
Transmission: Hydraulic. Voith L37U torque converter.
Weight: 57 tonnes.
Length: 10.75 m (35 ft 3 in).
Maximum Speed: 50 km/h (31 mph).

8301 LNC	8311 LNC	8317 LNC
8302 LNC	8312 LNC	8319 LNC
8303 LNC	8313 LNC	8320 LNC
8304 LNC	8314 LNC	8322 LNC
8305 LNC	8315 LNC	8323 LNC
8310 LNC	8316 LNC	8325 LNC

84 CLASS

Built: 1955-63 by ABR & BM. 8461-70 rebuilt 1968-79.
Engine: ABC 6DUS or 6DXS of 410 kW (550 hp) at 680 rpm.
Transmission: Hydraulic. Voith L37U torque converter.
Weight: 54.2-55.8 tonnes.
Length: 10.65 m (34 ft 11 in).
Maximum Speed: 50 km/h (31 mph).

8404 GMN	8430 FSD	8453 FNDM
8405 GMN	8431 FSD	8454 FNDM
8406 GMN	8432 FSD	8455 FNDM
8407 GMN	8433 GMN	8456 FNDM
8408 GMN	8434 FSD	8457 FNDM
8410 GT	8435 LK	8458 FNDM
8412 GMN	8437 FSD	8459 FNDM
8414 GMN	8439 LK	8460 FNDM
8415 GMN	8440 LK	8461 FNDM
8417 GT	8441 FSD	8462 FNDM
8418 MUT	8442 FNDM	8463 FNDM
8419 MUT	8443 LK	8464 FNDM
8421 MUT	8444 LK	8465 FNDM
8422 MUT	8447 GT	8466 FNDM
8424 GMN	8448 GT	8467 FNDM
8426 FSD	8449 GT	8468 FNDM
8427 MUT	8450 GT	8469 FNDM
8428 GT	8451 FNDM	8470 FNDM
8429 FSD	8452 FNDM	

85 CLASS

Built: 1956-57 by Forges, Usines et Fonderies.
Engine: ABC 6DXS of 410 kW (550 hp) at 680 rpm.
Transmission: Hydraulic. Voith L37U torque converter.
Weight: 58.5 tonnes.
Length: 10.00 m (32 ft 10 in).
Maximum Speed: 50 km/h (31 mph).

8501 FNDM	8506 FNDM	8511 FNDM
8502 FNDM	8507 FNDM	8512 FNDM
8503 FNDM	8508 FNDM	8513 FNDM
8504 FNDM	8509 FNDM	8514 FNDM
8505 FNDM	8510 FNDM	8515 FNDM

Top: SNCB 84 class no. 8435 at Kortrijk Depot on 29.12.89. *(D. Rowland)*

Bottom: SNCB 91 class no. 9139 at Antwerpen Dam Depot on 1st January 1990. *(D. Rowland)*

8516 FNDM	8520 FNDM	8523 FNDM
8517 FNDM	8521 FNDM	8524 FNDM
8518 FNDM	8522 FNDM	8525 FNDM
8519 FNDM		

91 CLASS   B

Built: 1961-64 by Cockerill, ABR & Niv.
Engine: General Motors 12V71N (two stroke) of 250kW (335 hp) at 1800 rpm.
Transmission: Hydraulic.
Weight: 36tonnes.
Length: 6.625 m (21 ft 9 in).
Maximum Speed: 45 km/h (28 mph).

9101 FGSP	9121 FSR	9141 FCR
9102 FGSP	9122 FMS	9142 FNR
9103 FGSP	9123 FKR	9143 FEO
9104 LK	9124 FMS	9144 FGH
9105 LK	9125 MKM	9145 MGR
9106 LK	9126 FGH	9146 FEO
9107 LK	9127 MKM	9147 FEO
9108 LK	9128 FMS	9148 MKM
9109 LK	9129 FNDM	9149 FEO
9110 LK	9130 FGH	9150 FWO
9111 FGH	9131 FGH	9151 FEO
9112 FGH	9132 FKR	9152 FKR
9113 FGH	9133 FGH	9153 MKM
9114 FGH	9134 MKM	9154 FNR
9115 FGH	9135 MKM	9155 FEO
9116 FEO	9136 FKR	9156 FEO
9117 FGH	9137 MKM	9157 FEO
9118 FGH	9138 FGSP	9158 FEO
9119 FSR	9139 FNDM	9159 MKM
9120 FGH	9140 LBC	9160 FKR

92 CLASS   C

Built: 1960 by BN.
Engine: SEM 6K113HS of 260 kW (350 hp) at 1300 rpm.
Transmission: Hydraulic. Voith L37 torque converter.
Weight: 50.6 tonnes.
Length: 10.40 m (34 ft 1 in).
Maximum Speed: 45 km/h (28 mph).

9201 FKR	9210 MGR	9218 FKR
9202 FFO	9211 MGR	9219 FNDM
9203 FGH	9212 FNDM	9220 FFO
9204 FNDM	9213 FEO	9221 FFO
9205 FHS	9214 LNC	9222 FHS
9206 MGR	9215 MGR	9223 FGH
9207 FEO	9216 LNC	9224 FEO
9208 FFO	9217 FEO	9225 FKR
9209 FKR		

SNCB 92 class no. 9205 at Leuven Depot on 30.10.89. *(D. Rowland)*

THE NETHERLANDS
Nederlandse Spoorwegen (NS).

Gauge: 1435 mm (4 ft 8 in).
Route Length: 2871 km.

Depots

Locomotives are not officially allocated to specific depots as in other countries, but major servicing work is carried out as follows: Electric Locomotives - Maastricht. Diesel Locomotives - Zwolle, Feijenoord (Rotterdam) and Watergraafsmeer (Amsterdam).

Other Depots & Stabling Points

Alkmaar, Almelo, Amersfoort, Amsterdam Dijksgracht, Amsterdam Zaanstraat, Arnhem, Botlek, Den Haag CS, Deventer, Dordrecht, Eindhoven, Enschede, Goes, Groningen, Haarlem, Heerlen, Hengelo, Hoek van Holland Haven, Kifjhoek Yard, Leeuwarden, Leidschendam, Nijmegen, Onnen, Roosendaal, Rotterdam CS, Rotterdam North Bank Harbour, Rotterdam North Goods, s' Hertogenbosch, Sittard, Susteren, Terneuzen, Utrecht, Venlo, Vlissingen, Waalhaven Zuid, Zutphen.

Works

Tilburg - All locomotives. A number of DMU & EMU vehicles are often also present.
Haarlem - EMU and coaching stock vehicles.
Onnen - All DMU and some EMU vehicles.

Railrover Information

7 Day Rail Rover: 7 consecutive days unlimited travel on all NS services. Prices: £33.50 2nd Class, £49.50 1st Class. No child reductions, although up to 3 children (4-11) can accompany each adult by each purchasing a "Railrunner" ticket for each day price 30p. Passport number details required for Rail Rovers.
1 Day Rail Rover: 1 day unlimited travel on all NS services. Price £15.50 2nd Class, £23.00 1st Class. Children should use Railrunner tickets (see above). Passport number details required.
Public Transport Link Rover: Available only in conjunction with the 1 and 7 Day Rail Rovers, this gives additional availability on all buses, trams & urban

metro systems throughout the country for the validity of the Rail Rover. Price: £1.70 (1 Day), £6.50 (7 days). Passport number details required.

Holland Railpass: 3 days unlimited travel on all NS services within a 15 consecutive day period. Prices: £24.00 2nd Class, £30.00 1st Class. Children (4-11) £1.00. Passport number details required.

Teenage Rover: Available during the months of June, July and August only to persons less than 19 years of age. 4 days unlimited travel on all NS services within a 10 consecutive days period. Price: £15.00 2nd Class only. Proof of age and passport number details required.

Teenage Rover Plus: A teenage rover as above, but with additional availability on all buses, trams & urban metro systems throughout the country on the days when validated for rail use. Price £18.50 2nd Class only.

Family Rover: Available during the months of June, July and August only to married couples or two persons who have lived at the same address for at least one year plus all their unmarried children under the age of 19 (includes step, foster and adopted children). 4 days unlimited travel on all NS services within a 10 consecutive days period. Price: £50.00 2nd Class, £62.00 1st Class, Proof of family relationship and a passport size photograph of each parent is required in addition to passport number details.

Family Rover Plus: A family rover as above, but with additional availability on all buses, trams & urban metro systems throughout the country on the days when validated for rail use. Price £62.00 2nd Class, £74.00 1st Class.

Multi-Rovers: A 1 Day Rover for 2-6 passengers travelling together (2 children 4-11 count as one adult). Available for use after 0900 on weekdays and all day on Saturdays, Sundays and Public Holidays. May also be used without restriction on any day in June, July or August. Prices shown are the cost per ticket, not per person. 2 passengers: £23.00 2nd Class, £35.00 1st Class. 3 passengers: £28.00 2nd Class, £42.00 1st Class. 4 passengers: £32.00 2nd Class, £47.00 1st Class. 5 passengers: £35.00 2nd Class, £53.00 1st Class. 6 passengers: £38.00 2nd Class, £59.00 1st Class. Passport number details required.

Benelux-Tourrail: 5 days unlimited travel on all SNCB/NMBS, NS & CFL services within a predetermined 17 day period. Prices: Adult (above 25) 2nd Class £43.50, 1st Class £65.00. Junior (4-25 years) £31.00 2nd Class, £46.00 1st Class. Passport number details required. Juniors will be required to have proof of age before tickets can be issued.

Tickets & Details: ABTA Travel Agents or Netherlands Railways, 25/28 Buckingham Gate, London, SW1E 6LD. (Tel: 01-630 1735 [until 06.05.90]; 071 630 1735 [from 07.05.90]). Access/Visa Cards are accepted and bookings for many tickets will be accepted by telephone.

Timetable: Valid for 1 year from May 1990, Price £2.00 + £1.00 postage and packing from the Netherlands Railways address above.

DIESEL SHUNTING LOCOMOTIVES

200 CLASS   Bo

Built: 1934-51 by Werkspoor/NS Zwolle.
Engine: Stork R153 of 63 kW (84 hp).
Transmission: Electric. Heemaf TM6 or Smit GT 322/7 traction motors.
Weight: 21 (*23) tonnes.
Length: 7.22 m (23 ft 8 in).
Maximum   Speed: 60 km/h (37 mph).
Notes: * Fitted with Hiab telescopic crane.

203	223	241	254	270	288
204	225	242*	255	271	289
209	226	243	256	274*	290
210	227*	244	257	276*	291
211	228	245	259	278	292
213	229	246*	260	279	296
214	230	247	262	281	297
215	231	248*	263	283	298
217	232	249	264	284*	299
218	234	250*	265*	285	300
219	235	252*	267	286	301
222	238	253			
302	Ut Oerske				
303	315	326	337	346	357
305	316	327	338	347	358
306	318	328	339	348	359
307	319	329	340	349	360*
308	320	330	341	350	361*
309*	321	331	342	351	362*
310	322	332	343	352	363
312	323	334	344	353	368*
313	324	335	345	355*	369
314	325	336			

600 CLASS   C

Built: 1955-56 by English Electric (Dick, Kerr).
Engine: English Electric 6KT of 294 kW (390 hp) at 680 rpm.
Transmission: Electric. Two English Electric 506/4B traction motors.
Weight: 47 tonnes.   **Length:** 9.01 m (29 ft 7 in).
Maximum   Speed: 30 km/h (19 mph).

Top: NS 200 class no. 209 at Roosendaal on 24.06.89.

(N. E. Webster/Metro Collection)

Bottom: NS 1100 class no. 1102 at Utrecht CS with an international service on 20.06.87. *(D. W. Fickes)*

601	612	623	634	645	656
602	613	624	635	646	657
603	614	625	636	647	658
604	615	626	637	648	659
605	616	627	638	649	660
606	617	628	639	650	661
607	618	629	640	651	662
608	619	630	641	652	663
609	620	631	642	653	664
610	621	632	643	654	665
611	622	633	644	655	

ELECTRIC LOCOMOTIVES

1100 CLASS   Bo-Bo

Built: 1950-56 by Alsthom. Rebuilt by NS Tilburg 1978-82.
Supply System: 1500 V dc overhead.
Traction Motors: Alsthom TA 628A.
Continuous rating: 1867 kW (2500 hp).
Weight: 83 tonnes.
Length: 14.18 m (46 ft 6 in).
Maximum Speed: 130 km/h (81 mph).

1101	1111	1123	1138	1150
1102	1112	1124	1139	1151
1103	1113	1127	1142	1152
1104	1114	1129	1143	1153
1105	1115	1130	1144	1154
1106	1116	1132	1145	1155
1107	1117	1134	1146	1157
1108	1119	1135	1147	1158
1109	1120	1136	1148	1159
1110	1122	1137	1149	1160

Note: 1120 entered Tilburg works for a possible overhaul late in 1989, being withdrawn prior to this. Whether or not this overhaul is carried out remains to be seen.

1200 CLASS

Co-Co

Built: 1950-56 by Werkspoor.
Supply System: 1500 V dc overhead.
Traction Motors: Heemaf TM 94.
Continuous rating: 2208 kW (2950 hp).
Weight: 108 tonnes.
Length: 18.09 m (59 ft 4 in).
Maximum Speed: 130 km/h (81 mph).

1201	1206	1211	1216	1222
1202	1207	1212	1217	1223
1203	1208	1213	1218	1224
1204	1209	1214	1219	1225
1205	1210	1215	1221	

1300 CLASS

Co-Co

Built: 1952-56 by Alsthom.
Supply System: 1500 V dc overhead.
Traction Motors: Alsthom TA628A.
Continuous rating: 2850 kW (3810 hp).
Weight: 111 tonnes.
Length: 18.95 m (62 ft 2 in).
Maximum Speed: 135 km/h (84 mph).

1301	Dieren	1310	Bussum
1302	Woerden	1311	Best
1304		1312	Zoetermeer
1305	Alphen aan der Rijn	1313	Nunspeet
1306	Brummen	1314	Hoorn
1307		1315	Tiel
1308		1316	Geldermalsen
1309			

1600 CLASS

B-B

Built: 1980-83 by Alsthom.
Supply System: 1500 V dc overhead.
Traction Motors: Two Alsthom Atlantique TAB 674 C4.
Continuous rating: 4340 kW (5810 hp).
Weight: 84 tonnes.   **Length:** 17.64 m (57 ft 9 in).
Maximum Speed: 160 km/h (100 mph).

1601	Amsterdam	1630	Zwolle
1602	Schipol	1631	Voorburg
1603	Zutphen	1632	Nijmegen
1604	Dordrecht	1633	Bergen op Zoom
1605	Breda	1634	Lelystad
1606	Harderwijk	1635	Enschede
1607	Vlissingen	1636	Heerenveen
1608	s'Hertogenbosch	1637	Amersfoort
1609	Hoofddorp	1638	Groningen
1610	Hengelo	1639	Leiden
1611	Venlo	1640	Steenwijk
1612	Goes	1641	Almere
1613	Roermond	1642	Weert
1614	Schiedam	1643	Heerlen
1615	Zandvoort	1644	Roosendaal
1616	Oldenzaal	1645	Middelburg
1617	Assen	1646	Leeuwarden
1618	Almelo	1647	Delft
1619	Maastricht	1648	Valkenburg
1620	Arnhem	1649	Oss
1621	Deventer	1650	Den Haag
1622	Haarlem	1651	Tilburg
1623	Hilversum	1652	Utrecht
1624	Alkmaar	1653	Den Helder
1625	Sittard	1654	Geleen
1626	Meppel	1655	Eindhoven
1627	Gouda	1656	Hoogeveen
1628	Apeldoorn	1657	Rotterdam
1629	Ede	1658	Zaandam

1700 CLASS   B-B

Built: 1991 onwards by Alsthom.
Supply System: 1500 V dc overhead.
Traction Motors:
Continuous rating:
Weight: tonnes.
Length: m (ft in).
Maximum Speed: 160 km/h (100 mph).

Top: NS 1200 class no. 1205 stabled at Hoek Van Holland Haven on 20.06.87.
(D. W. Fickes)

Bottom: NS 1300 class no. 1301 approaches Utrecht CS with a heavy freight.
(N. E. Webster)

1701	1720			
1702	1721			
1703	1722			
1704	1723			
1705	1724			
1706	1725			
1707	1726			
1708	1727			
1709	1728			
1710	1729			
1711	1730			
1712	1731			
1713	1732			
1714	1733			
1715	1734			
1716	1735			
1717	1736			
1718	1737			
1719	1738			

DIESEL MAIN LINE LOCOMOTIVES

2200 CLASS   Bo-Bo

Built: 1955-58 by Allan (2201-2300) or Schneider (2301-48)
Engine: Stork/Schneider Superior 40C-Lx-8 of 662 kW (880 hp) at 1100 rpm.
Transmission: Electric. Heemaf TM98 traction motors.
Weight: 72 tonnes.
Length: 14.01 m (46 ft).
Maximum Speed: 100 km/h (62 mph).

2201	2213	2225	2243	2256
2202	2214	2226	2244	2257
2203	2215	2228	2245	2258
2204	2216	2229	2246	2259
2205	2217	2230	2247	2260
2207	2219	2234	2249	2261
2208	2220	2235	2250	2263
2209	2221	2236	2251	2264
2210	2222	2238	2253	2266
2211	2223	2239	2254	2267
2212	2224	2241	2255	2268

2269	2284	2298	2310	2329
2270	2285	2299	2311	2330
2271	2286	2300	2317	2332
2272	2289	2301	2318	2333
2273	2290	2302	2319	2335
2274	2291	2303	2320	2336
2275	2292	2304	2322	2338
2276	2293	2305	2323	2339
2277	2294	2306	2324	2342
2278	2295	2307	2326	2344
2280	2296	2308	2327	2346
2282	2297	2309	2328	2348
2283				

2400 CLASS   Bo-Bo

Built: 1954-56 by Alsthom.
Engine: SACM V12 SHR 625 kW (830 hp) at 1500 rpm.
Transmission: Electric. Alsthom TA 637 traction motors.
Weight: 60 tonnes.
Length: 12.52 m (41 ft 1 in).
Maximum Speed: 80 km/h (50 mph).

2405	2423	2446	2458	2501
2406	2424	2447	2462	2502
2407	2425	2449	2463	2504
2412	2434	2450	2465	2506
2413	2435	2452	2467	2510
2414	2439	2453	2470	2513
2418	2443	2454	2477	2526
2419	2444	2456	2482	2528

6400 CLASS   Bo-Bo

Built: 1987 onwards by MaK. In the course of delivery. 6401-30 had been delivered by the end of 1989.
Engine: MTU 12V 396 TC 13 of 1180 kW (1575 hp) at 1800 rpm.
Transmission: Three Phase Electric. BBC traction motors.
Weight: 80 tonnes.
Length: 14.40 m (47 ft 3 in).
Maximum Speed: 120 km/h (75 mph).

6401	Mijndert	6446	
6402	Marinus	6447	
6403	Gijs	6448	
6404	Johan	6449	
6405	Jan	6450	
6406	Tonnie	6451	
6407	Henk	6452	
6408	Gerard	6453	
6409	Herman	6454	
6410	Toon	6455	
6411	Oliver	6456	
6412	Hans	6457	
6413	Foeke	6458	
6414	Sander	6459	
6415	Rens	6460	
6416		6461	
6417		6462	
6418	Inge	6463	
6419		6464	
6420		6465	
6421		6466	
6422	Wim	6467	
6423		6468	
6424		6469	
6425		6470	
6426		6471	
6427		6472	
6428		6473	
6429		6474	
6430		6475	
6431		6476	
6432		6477	
6433		6478	
6434		6479	
6435		6480	
6436		6481	
6437		6482	
6438		6483	
6439		6484	
6440		6485	
6441		6486	
6442		6487	
6443		6488	
6444		6489	
6445		6490	

6491	6506
6492	6507
6493	6508
6494	6509
6495	6510
6496	6511
6497	6512
6498	6513
6499	6514
6500	6515
6501	6516
6502	6517
6503	6518
6504	6519
6505	6520

NS 2400 class no. 2501 still sports its original Victoria Brown livery (albeit retouched and minus original numberplate) to this day. It is seen here at Nijmegen on 05.05.88. *(D. W. Fickes)*

FRANCE
Société National des Chemins de Fer Français (SNCF).

Gauges: 1435 mm (4 ft 8ᐟ in); 1000 mm (3 ft 3.37 in).
Route Length: 34568 km (1435 mm); 99 km (1000 mm).

Depots

Depots with a locomotive allocation are as follows:

ACH	Achères (Paris)
AVI	Avignon
BEZ	Béziers
BOR	Bordeaux
CAN	Caen
CBY	Chambéry
CLY	Chalindrey
DIJ	Dijon Perrigny
HEN	Hendaye
LAB	Les Aubrais (Orléans)
LIM	Limoges
LEN	Lens
LMS	Le Mans
LON	Longueau (Amiens)
LYM	Lyon Mouche
LYV	Lyon Vaise
MAR	Marseille Blancarde
MET	Metz
MOH	Mohon (Charleville-Mézièrs)
MON	Montrouge (Paris)
NAN	Nantes
NEV	Nevers
NIM	Nîmes
PLC	Paris La Chapelle
PLP	Paris La Plaine
PLV	Paris La Villette
PSO	Paris Sud Ouest
REN	Rennes
SOT	Sotteville (Rouen)
STR	Strasbourg
TAR	Tarbes

THI	Thionville
TOU	Toulouse
TSP	Tours St. Pierre
VEN	Venissieux (Lyon)
VLG	Villefranche-le-Conflent
VSG	Villeneuve St. Georges (Paris)

Other Depots & Stabling Points

Aix-les-Bains, Amberieu, Amiens, Angers, Angloueme, Annemasse, Argentan, Aulnoye, Auray, Aurillac, Batignolles, Bayonne, Belfort, Bellegarde, Blainville, Bobigny, Boissy-St. Leger, Boulogne Ville, Bourg, Bourges, Bresançon, Brest, Bretigny, Brieoc, Brive, Calais Ville, Cannes La Bocca, Capdenac, Cerbère, Chasse Triage, Chateauroux, Chatres, Chaumont, Cherbourg, Clermont-Ferrand, Conflans Jarny, Creil Petit Therain, Creil Ville, Culoz, Dieppe, Dijon Gevrey, Dijon Ville, Dôle, Douai, Dunkerque Grande Synthe, Grenoble, Epinal, Étampes, Hausbergen, Juvisy, La Rochelle, La Rochelle Ville, Laroche Migennes, Lauterbourg, Le Havre, Le Mans Triage, Lille Fives, Lille La Deliverance, Longwy, Lumes, Lyon Perrache, Mantes La Jolie, Marsailles St. Charles, Massy Paliseau, Melun, Mirimas, Mitry Claye, Modane, Montargis, Montluçon, Moret les Sablons, Mulhouse Ville, Mulhouse Nord, Nancy, Nanterre Universite, Narbonne, Neufchateau, Neussargues, Nice St. Rochelle, Noisy-le-Sec, Paris Chatillon, Paris Les Ardoines, Paris Lyon (Charlois), Paris Sud Est, Paris St. Lazare, Pau, Perigneaux, Perpignan, Persan Beaumont, Poitiers, Pontoise, Portes, Quimper, Reims, Roanne, Rodez, Rueil-Malmaison, St. Cloud, St. Etienne, St. Germain des Fosses, St. Gervais-les-Bains, St. Jean de Maurienne, Saintes, Sarreinsming, Sibelin Triage, Somain, Tergnier, Thouars, Trappes, Valenciennes, Valenton, Vaires, Versailles, Veynes, Vierzon, Villefranche-le-Conflent, Vitry (Paris), Woippy.

Works

Beziérs - BB 300, CC 1100, BB 4200, BB 4700, BB 8000, BB9400, emus.
Bischeim   (Strasbourg): TGV.
Bordeaux: DMU. Épernay: BB 12000, BB 16500.
Hellemmes   (Lille): BB 15000, BB 16000, BB 17000, BB 20200, BB 25100, BB 25150, BB 25200, CC 40100.
La Folie   (Paris): EMU. Le **Mans:** DMU.
Nevers: BB 63400, BB 63500, BB 66000, BB 66400, BB 66600, BB 66700, BB 67000, BB 67200, BB 67300, Y 2400, Y 5100, Y 7100, Y 7400, Y 8000.
Oullins   (Lyon): CC 6500, BB 7200, BB 9200, BB 9300, CC 21000, BB 22200, BB 25500, DMU.
Quatre   Mares   (Sotteville): BB 63000, BB 67400, A1AA1A 68000, A1AA1A 68500, CC 72000.
Vitry   (Paris): EMU.

Railrover Information

France Vacances Pass: 4 days unlimited travel on all SNCF services (excluding Corsica) within a fixed 15 day period. Prices: £75.00 2nd Class, £103.00 1st Class. Children (4-11) 50% reduction. Passport number details required. 9 days unlimited travel on all SNCF services (excluding Corsica) within a fixed one month period. Prices: £127.00 2nd Class, £185.00 1st Class. Children (4-11) 50% reduction. Passport number details required. In addition all France Vacance Passes offer a range of other discounts and facilities, including a £14.00 single fare on Hoverspeed, 50% reduction on the Chemins de Fer de Provence Line and concessions on the Paris Metro and buses. Full details are available at the time of booking.

Tickets & Details: ABTA Travel Agents or French Railways Ltd., French Railways House, 179 Piccadilly, London, W1V 0BA. Tel: 01-493-9731. Tickets are also available from certain British Rail Travel Centres.

ELECTRIC LOCOMOTIVES

Special Note: Many SNCF locomotives are fitted with monomotor bogies which offer the driver a choice of two sets of gear ratios according to the type of trains to be worked. In this publication the first figure quoted in the performance details relates to the low gear ratio (freight work) and the second to the high gear ratio (passenger work).

BB 300 CLASS   Bo-Bo

Built: 1938-39 by Siemens/Alsthom.
Supply System: 1500 V dc overhead.
Continuous rating: 1240 kW (1660 hp).
Weight: 80 tonnes.
Length: 12.93 m (42 ft 5 in).
Maximum Speed: 75 km/h (47 mph).

301 PSO	310 PSO	317 VEN
302 CBY	311 VSG	319 PSO
304 PSO	312 LIM	320 VEN
305 PSO	313 VEN	321 PSO
307 VSG	314 PSO	322 PSO
308 PSO	315 PSO	323 PSO
309 CBY	316 PSO	324 PSO

Top: Elderly SNCF electrics BB 4206 & BB 4757 head a row of sister locos at Paris Sud Ouest Depot on 22.02.88. *(R. G. Morris)*

Bottom: SNCF CC 6500 class no. CC 6542 heads a car train through Aix Les Bains on 13.07.83. *(D. W. Fickes)*

BB 325 CLASS
Bo-Bo

Built: 1946-39 by Alsthom/Schneider-Jeumont.
Supply System: 1500 V dc overhead.
Continuous rating: 1240 kW (1660 hp).
Weight: 80 tonnes.
Length: 12.93 m (42 ft 5 in).
Maximum Speed: 75 km/h (47 mph).

327 AVI	340 VEN	348 DIJ
328 VEN	342 VEN	349 VSG
331 VEN	343 VEN	350 VEN
333 VSG	344 VEN	351 VEN
334 VEN	345 AVI	353 VSG
335 VEN	346 AVI	354 VSG
336 VSG	347 DIJ	355 VSG
337 VEN		

CC 1100 CLASS
C-C

Built: 1937-48 by CGC/Oerlikon.
Supply System: 1500 V dc overhead.
Continuous rating: 400 kW (535 hp).
Weight: 91 tonnes.
Length: 17.91 m (58 ft 9 in).
Maximum Speed: 25 km/h (16 mph).

1101 VSG	1105 VSG	1109 TSP
1102 TSP	1106 TOU	1110 VSG
1103 TOU	1107 VSG	1111 TSP
1104 VSG	1108 TOU	1112 TOU

BB 4200 CLASS
Bo-Bo

Built: 1933-35 by Carel et Fouché/Alsthom.
Supply System: 1500 V dc overhead.
Continuous rating: 1160 kW (1550 hp).
Weight: 75 tonnes.
Length: 12.87 m (42 ft 3 in).
Maximum Speed: 75 km/h (47 mph).

4206 PSO	4226 TOU	4240 TOU
4208 TOU	4228 TOU	4242 TOU
4209 TOU	4231 TSP	4245 PSO
4211 PSO	4234 PSO	4246 TSP
4221 TOU	4239 PSO	4249 TOU
4224 PSO		

BB 4700 CLASS   Bo-Bo

Built: 1933-35 by Alsthom.
Supply System: 1500 V dc overhead.
Continuous rating: 1160 kW (1550 hp).
Weight: 75 tonnes.
Length: 12.87 m (42 ft 3 in).
Maximum Speed: 90 km/h (56 mph).

4730 TAR	4747 PSO	4762 LAB
4732 TSP	4749 LAB	4763 LAB
4733 BOR	4750 LAB	4764 PSO
4734 BOR	4752 TSP	4765 PSO
4735 BOR	4753 TSP	4767 LAB
4736 TAR	4754 PSO	4769 MON
4737 TAR	4755 PSO	4770 MON
4738 TAR	4756 LAB	4771 LIM
4739 LIM	4757 PSO	4772 LIM
4740 LAB	4758 LAB	4773 MON
4741 TSP	4759 PSO	4774 LAB
4743 TSP	4760 PSO	4775 MON
4745 LAB	4761 TSP	

CLASS CC 6500   C-C

Built: 1969-75 by Alsthom/MTE.
Supply System: 1500 V dc overhead.
Continuous rating: 5900 kW (7910 hp).
Weight: 116 tonnes.
Length: 20.19 m (66 ft 3 in).
Maximum Speed: 100/220 km/h (62/137 mph).

No.		Name	No.		Name
6501	LYM		6520	PSO	Ruffec
6502	PSO	Ivry-sur-Seine	6521	PSO	Saintes
6503	PSO		6522	PSO	Limoges
6504	PSO	Vitry-sur-Seine	6523	PSO	Brive
6505	PSO		6524	PSO	Toulouse
6506	PSO	Vierzon	6525	PSO	Châteauroux
6507	PSO	Sainte-Foy-La-Grande	6526	PSO	Choisy-Le-Roi
6508	PSO	Montauban	6527	PSO	Amboise
6509	PSO	Agen	6528	PSO	Luchon
6510	PSO	Carcassonne	6529	PSO	Issoudun
6511	PSO	Pamiers	6530	PSO	Cahors
6512	PSO	Narbonne	6531	PSO	Saint-Pierre-des-Corps
6513	PSO	Cognac	6532	PSO	
6514	PSO	Poitiers	6533	PSO	Beautiran
6515	PSO	Blois	6534	PSO	Béziers
6516	PSO	Châtellerault	6535	PSO	Saint-Chamond
6517	PSO	Arcachon	6536	PSO	Annecy
6518	PSO	Orléans	6537	PSO	Salon-de-Provence
6519	PSO	Angoulême	6538	PSO	

No.		No.		No.	
6539	PSO	6546	LYM	6553	LYM
6540	LYM	6547	LYM	6554	LYM
6541	LYM	6548	LYM	6555	LYM
6542	LYM	6549	LYM	6556	LYM
6543	LYM	6550	LYM	6557	LYM
6544	LYM	6551	LYM	6558	LYM
6545	LYM	6552	LYM	6559	LYM

No.		Name	No.		Name
6560	LYM	Oullins	6568	LYM	
6561	LYM		6569	LYM	La Mulatière
6562	LYM		6570	LYM	Armentières
6563	LYM	Laval	6571	LYM	Jeumont
6564	LYM	Beaune	6572	LYM	Résistance-Fer
6565	LYM		6573	PSO	Libourne
6566	LYM	Mauberge	6574	PSO	Dôle
6567	LYM	Brest			

CC 7000 CLASS   Co-Co

Built: 1949 by Alsthom/Fives-Lille.
Supply System: 1500 V dc overhead.
Continuous rating: 2770 kW (3710 hp).
Weight: 104 tonnes.   **Length:** 18.83 m (61 ft 9 in).
Maximum Speed: 150 km/h (93 mph).

No.		No.	
7001	AVI	7002	AVI

CC 7100 CLASS

Co-Co

Built: 1952-55 by Alsthom/Fives-Lille/MTE.
Supply System: 1500 V dc overhead.
Continuous rating: 3490 kW (4680 hp).[*3240 kW (4340 hp)]
Weight: 107 (*106) tonnes.
Length: 18.92 m (62 ft 1 in).
Maximum Speed: 150 km/h (93 mph).

7101 AVI(Z)	7120 AVI	7140 AVI
7102 AVI	7121 AVI	7141 AVI
7103 AVI	7122 AVI(Z)	7142 AVI(Z)
7105 AVI	7123 AVI	7143 AVI
7106 AVI(Z)	7124 AVI	7144* AVI
7107 AVI	7125 AVI	7145* AVI(Z)
7109 AVI	7126 AVI	7146* AVI
7110 AVI	7128 AVI	7149* AVI(Z)
7111 AVI(Z)	7130 AVI	7151* AVI
7112 AVI	7132 AVI	7152* AVI
7113 AVI	7134 AVI(Z)	7153* AVI
7115 AVI	7135 AVI	7154* AVI
7116 AVI	7136 AVI	7155* AVI
7117 AVI	7137 AVI	7157* AVI
7118 AVI	7138 AVI	7158* AVI
7119 AVI	7139 AVI(Z)	

BB 7200 CLASS

B-B

Built: 1976-85 by Alsthom/MTE.
Supply System: 1500 V dc overhead.
Continuous rating: 4360 kW (5845 hp).
Weight: 84 tonnes.
Length: 17.48 m (57 ft 4 in).
Maximum Speed: 180 km/h (112 mph) [*100 km/h (62 mph)].

7201* LIM	7202* LIM	
7203* LIM Saint-Flour		
7204* LIM	7211* LIM	7216* LIM
7205* LIM	7212* LIM	7217* LIM
7206* LIM	7213* LIM	7218* LIM
7207* LIM	7214* LIM	7219* LIM
7208* LIM	7215* LIM	7220* LIM
7210* LIM		

7221* LIM	Saint-Amand-Montrand	7222* LIM
7223* LIM	La Souterraine	
7224* LIM	7228* LIM	7232* LIM
7225* LIM	7229* LIM	7233* LIM
7226* LIM	7230* LIM	7234* LIM
7227* LIM	7231* LIM	7235* LIM
7236 PSO	Chambèry	7241 PSO	Villeurbanne
7237 PSO	Pierrelatte	7242 PSO	Vienne
7238 PSO	Thonon-Les-Bains	7243 PSO	Villeneuve-Saint-Georges
7239 PSO	Saint-Pierre-d'Albigny	7244 PSO	Vernou-La-Celle-surSeine
7240 PSO	Saint Etienne	7245 PSO	

7246 PSO	7249 PSO	7251 PSO
7247 PSO	7250 PSO	7252 PSO
7248 PSO		

7253 PSO	Montréjeau	7255 PSO
7254 PSO		7256 PSO	Valenton

7257 PSO	7282 VSG	7307 VSG
7258 PSO	7283 VSG	7308 VSG
7259 PSO	7284 VSG	7309 VSG
7260 PSO	7285 VSG	7310 VSG
7261 PSO	7286 VSG	7311 VSG
7262 PSO	7287 VSG	7312 VSG
7263 PSO	7288 VSG	7313 VSG
7264 VSG	7289 VSG	7314 VSG
7265 VSG	7290 VSG	7315 VSG
7266 VSG	7291 VSG	7316 VSG
7267 VSG	7292 VSG	7317 VSG
7268 VSG	7293 VSG	7318 VSG
7269 VSG	7294 VSG	7319 VSG
7270 VSG	7295 VSG	7320 VSG
7271 VSG	7296 VSG	7321 VSG
7272 VSG	7297 VSG	7322 VSG
7273 VSG	7298 VSG	7323 VSG
7274 VSG	7299 VSG	7324 VSG
7275 VSG	7300 VSG	7325 VSG
7276 VSG	7301 VSG	7326 VSG
7277 VSG	7302 VSG	7327 VSG
7278 VSG	7303 VSG	7328 VSG
7279 VSG	7304 VSG	7329 VSG
7280 VSG	7305 VSG	7330 VSG
7281 VSG	7306 VSG	7331 VSG

Top: SNCF CC 7100 class no. CC 7102 stands in sidings at Utrecht (Holland) during its visit for the NS150 celebrations in July 1989.   (N. E. Webster/Metro Collection)

Bottom: SNCF BB 8100 class no. BB 8187 at Culoz stabling point on 07.07.89
(D. J. Glossop)

7332 VSG	7358* CBY	7384 VSG
7333 VSG	7359* CBY	7385 VSG
7334 VSG	7360* CBY	7386 VSG
7335 VSG	7361* CBY	7387 VSG
7336 VSG	7362* CBY	7388 VSG
7337 VSG	7363* CBY	7389 VSG
7338 VSG	7364* CBY	7390 VSG
7339 VSG	7365* CBY	7391 VSG
7340 VSG	7366* CBY	7392 VSG
7341 VSG	7367* CBY	7393 VSG
7342 VSG	7368* CBY	7394 VSG
7343* CBY	7369* CBY	7395 VSG
7344* CBY	7370* CBY	7396 VSG
7345* CBY	7371* CBY	7397 VSG
7346* CBY	7372* CBY	7398 VSG
7347* CBY	7373* CBY	7399 VSG
7348* CBY	7374* CBY	7400 VSG
7349* CBY	7375* CBY	7401 VSG
7350* CBY	7376* CBY	7402 VSG
7351* CBY	7377* CBY	7403 VSG
7352* CBY	7378* CBY	7404 VSG
7353* CBY	7379* CBY	7405 VSG
7354* CBY	7380* CBY	7406 VSG
7355* CBY	7381 VSG	7407 VSG
7356* CBY	7382 VSG	7408 VSG
7357* CBY	7383 VSG	7409 VSG

7410 VSG	Fontenay-sous-bois
7411* CBY	Lamure-sur-Azergues

7412* CBY	7422* CBY	7432* CBY
7413* CBY	7423* CBY	7433* CBY
7414* CBY	7424* CBY	7434* CBY
7415* CBY	7425* CBY	7435* CBY
7416* CBY	7426* CBY	7436* CBY
7417* CBY	7427* CBY	7437* CBY
7418* CBY	7428* CBY	7438* CBY
7419* CBY	7429* CBY	7439* CBY
7420* CBY	7430* CBY	7440* CBY
7421* CBY	7431* CBY	

BB 8000 CLASS

B-B

Built: 1947-55 by Alsthom/Schneider-Jeumont/CGC/Siemens/Oerlikon.
Supply System: 1500 V dc overhead.
Continuous rating: 2100 kW (2815 hp).
Weight: 92 tonnes.
Length: 12.93 m (42 ft 5 in).
Maximum Speed: 105 km/h (65 mph).

8001 AVI	8134 DIJ	8168 DIJ
8101 AVI	8135 DIJ	8169 AVI
8102 AVI	8136 DIJ	8170 AVI
8103 AVI	8137 DIJ	8171 DIJ
8104 AVI(Z)	8138 DIJ	8172 DIJ
8105 AVI	8139 AVI	8173 DIJ
8106 AVI	8140 AVI	8174 DIJ
8107 AVI(Z)	8141 AVI	8175 DIJ
8108 AVI	8142 DIJ	8176 DIJ
8109 AVI	8143 DIJ	8177 AVI
8110 AVI	8144 AVI	8178 DIJ
8111 AVI	8145 DIJ	8179 AVI
8112 AVI	8146 AVI	8180 DIJ
8113 AVI	8147 AVI	8181 AVI
8114 AVI	8148 DIJ	8182 AVI
8115 AVI	8149 AVI	8183 AVI
8116 AVI(Z)	8150 AVI	8184 AVI
8117 AVI	8151 AVI	8185 DIJ
8118 AVI	8152 AVI	8186 DIJ
8119 AVI(Z)	8153 DIJ	8187 DIJ
8120 AVI	8154 AVI	8188 DIJ
8121 AVI	8155 DIJ	8189 AVI
8122 DIJ	8156 DIJ	8190 DIJ
8123 AVI	8157 DIJ	8191 DIJ
8124 AVI	8158 AVI	8192 DIJ
8125 DIJ	8159 DIJ	8193 DIJ
8126 AVI	8160 DIJ	8194 AVI
8127 DIJ(Z)	8161 AVI	8195 DIJ
8128 AVI	8162 AVI	8196 DIJ
8129 AVI	8163 AVI	8197 DIJ
8130 DIJ	8164 DIJ	8198 DIJ
8131 DIJ	8165 AVI	8199 DIJ
8132 DIJ	8166 AVI	8200 AVI
8133 DIJ(Z)	8167 DIJ	8201 DIJ

8202 DIJ(Z)	8224 DIJ	8246 DIJ
8203 DIJ	8225 DIJ(Z)	8247 AVI
8204 DIJ	8226 DIJ	8248 AVI
8205 AVI	8227 DIJ	8249 DIJ
8206 DIJ	8228 AVI	8250 DIJ
8207 DIJ	8229 DIJ	8251 AVI
8208 DIJ	8230 AVI	8252 AVI
8209 DIJ	8231 DIJ	8253 DIJ
8210 DIJ	8232 DIJ	8256 DIJ
8211 DIJ	8233 DIJ	8257 DIJ(Z)
8212 DIJ	8234 AVI	8258 AVI
8213 DIJ(Z)	8235 DIJ	8259 AVI
8214 DIJ	8236 DIJ	8263 DIJ
8215 DIJ	8237 DIJ	8264 DIJ
8216 DIJ	8238 DIJ(Z)	8265 DIJ
8217 DIJ	8239 DIJ	8266 AVI
8218 DIJ	8240 AVI	8267 DIJ(Z)
8219 AVI	8241 DIJ	8268 DIJ(Z)
8220 DIJ	8242 AVI	8269 AVI
8221 AVI	8243 DIJ(Z)	8270 DIJ
8222 AVI	8244 DIJ(Z)	8271 DIJ(Z)
8223 DIJ	8245 DIJ	

BB 8500 CLASS   B-B

Built: 1964-74 by Alsthom.
Supply System: 1500 V dc overhead.
Continuous rating: 2610 kW (3490 hp)[*+ 2940 kW (3940 hp)].
Weight: 78 (*79, +80) tonnes.
Length: 14.70 m (48 ft 3 in) [* 14.94 m (49 ft); + 15.57 m (51 ft 1 in)].
Maximum Speed: 90/140 km/h (56/87 mph).

8501 LAB	8512 LAB	8523 LAB
8502 LAB	8513 LAB	8524 LAB
8503 LAB	8514 LAB	8525 LAB
8504 LAB	8515 LAB	8526 LAB
8505 LAB	8516 LAB	8527 LAB
8506 LAB	8517 LAB	8528 LAB
8507 LAB	8518 LAB	8529 LAB
8508 LAB	8519 LAB	8530 LAB
8509 LAB	8520 LAB	8531 LAB
8510 LAB	8521 LAB	8532 LAB
8511 LAB	8522 LAB	8533 LAB

8534 LAB	8556* MON	8578* VEN
8535 LAB	8557* MON	8579* VEN
8536 LAB	8558* MON	8580* TOU
8537* LAB	8559* MON	8581* MON
8538* LAB	8560* VSG	8582* VEN
8539* LAB	8561* VSG	8583* TOU
8540* TOU	8562* MON	8584* TOU
8541* LAB	8563* VSG	8585* MON
8542* LAB	8564* VSG	8586* TOU
8543* LAB	8565* VEN	8587* TOU
8544* TOU	8566* VSG	8588+ MON
8545* VSG	8567* VEN	8589+ MON
8546* MON	8568* MON	8590+ MON
8547* MON	8569* MON	8591+ MON
8548* MON	8570* VEN	8592+ MON
8549* TOU	8571* VEN	8593+ MON
8550* VSG	8572* TOU	8594+ MON
8551* TOU	8573* VEN	8595+ MON
8552* MON	8574* VEN	8596+ MON
8553* MON	8575* TOU	8597+ MON
8554* MON	8576* TOU	8598+ MON
8555* VSG	8577* VEN	8599+ MON

8600+ TOU	Fluery-Les Aubrais
8601+ TOU	Ax-Les-Thermes
8602+ TOU	Foix
8603+ TOU	Lannemezan
8604+ TOU	Cerdagne
8605+ TOU	Saint-Gaudens

8606+ TOU	8620+ TOU	8634+ TOU
8607+ TOU	8621+ TOU	8635+ TOU
8608+ TOU	8622+ TOU	8636+ TOU
8609+ TOU	8623+ TOU	8637+ TOU
8610+ TOU	8624+ TOU	8638+ TOU
8611+ TOU	8625+ TOU	8639+ TOU
8612+ TOU	8626+ TOU	8640+ TOU
8613+ TOU	8627+ TOU	8641+ TOU
8614+ TOU	8628+ TOU	8642+ TOU
8615+ TOU	8629+ TOU	8643+ MON
8616+ TOU	8630+ TOU	8644+ TOU
8617+ TOU	8631+ TOU	8645+ MON
8618+ TOU	8632+ TOU	8646+ MON
8619+ TOU	8633+ TOU	

BB 9200 CLASS   Bo-Bo

Built: 1957-64 by Schneider-Jeumont/CEM
Supply System: 1500 V dc overhead.
Continuous rating: 3850 kW (5160 hp).
Weight: 82 tonnes.
Length: 16.20 m (53 ft 2 in).
Maximum Speed: 160 km/h (100 mph).

9201 BOR	9217 BOR	9233 BOR
9202 BOR	9218 BOR	9234 BOR
9203 BOR	9219 BOR	9235 BOR
9204 BOR	9220 BOR	9236 BOR
9205 BOR	9221 BOR	9237 BOR
9206 BOR	9222 BOR	9238 BOR
9207 BOR	9223 BOR	9239 PSO
9208 BOR	9224 BOR	9240 PSO
9209 BOR	9225 BOR	9241 PSO
9210 BOR	9226 BOR	9242 PSO
9211 BOR	9227 BOR	9243 PSO
9212 BOR	9228 BOR	9244 PSO
9213 BOR	9229 BOR	9245 PSO
9214 BOR	9230 BOR	9246 PSO
9215 BOR	9231 BOR	9247 PSO
9216 BOR	9232 BOR	

9248 PSO La-Teste-de-Buch		
9250 PSO	9260 PSO	9270 PSO
9251 PSO	9261 PSO	9271 PSO
9252 PSO	9262 PSO	9272 PSO
9253 PSO	9263 PSO	9273 PSO
9254 PSO	9264 PSO	9274 PSO
9255 PSO	9265 PSO	9275 PSO
9256 PSO	9266 PSO	9276 PSO
9257 PSO	9267 PSO	9277 PSO
9258 PSO	9268 PSO	9278 PSO
9259 PSO	9269 PSO	9279 PSO

9280 PSO Arpajon		
9281 PSO	9285 PSO	9289 PSO
9282 PSO	9286 PSO	9290 PSO
9283 PSO	9287 PSO	9291 PSO
9284 PSO	9288 PSO	9292 PSO

BB 9300 CLASS   Bo-Bo

Built: 1967-69 by Schneider-Jeumont/CEM/MTE.
Supply System: 1500 V dc overhead.
Continuous rating: 3850 kW (5160 hp).
Weight: 84 tonnes.
Length: 16.20 m (53 ft 2 in).
Maximum Speed: 160 km/h (100 mph).

9301 TOU	9310 TOU	9318 TOU
9302 TOU	9311 TOU	9319 TOU
9303 TOU	9312 TOU	9320 TOU
9304 TOU	9313 TOU	9321 TOU
9305 TOU	9314 TOU	9322 TOU
9306 TOU	9315 TOU	9323 TOU
9307 TOU	9316 TOU	9324 TOU
9308 TOU	9317 TOU	9325 TOU
9309 TOU		

9326 TOU	Montrabe	
9327 TOU		
9329 TOU	Castres	9328 TOU
9330 TOU	9334 TOU	9338 TOU
9331 TOU	9335 TOU	9339 TOU
9332 TOU	9336 TOU	9340 TOU
9333 TOU	9337 TOU	

BB 9400 CLASS   B-B

Built: 1967-69 by Fives-Lille/MTE/CEM
Supply System: 1500 V dc overhead.
Continuous rating: 2210 kW (2965 hp).
Weight: 60 tonnes.
Length: 14.40 m (47 ft 3 in).
Maximum Speed: 130 km/h (81 mph).

9401 BOR(Z)	9409 BOR	9418 BOR(Z)
9403 BOR	9410 BOR	9419 BOR
9404 BOR	9411 BOR	9421 BOR
9405 AVI	9412 BOR	9422 BOR
9406 BOR	9413 BOR	9423 BOR
9407 BOR(Z)	9415 BOR	9424 BOR
9408 BOR	9416 BOR	9425 BOR

9426 BOR	9461 AVI	9499 AVI
9429 BOR	9462 AVI	9500 AVI
9430 BOR(Z)	9464 AVI	9503 AVI
9433 BOR	9466 AVI	9504 AVI(Z)
9434 BOR	9467 AVI	9505 AVI
9435 BOR	9468 AVI	9506 AVI
9436 BOR	9470 AVI	9507 AVI
9437 BOR	9471 AVI	9508 AVI
9438 BOR	9473 AVI (Z)	9509 AVI(Z)
9439 BOR	9474 AVI	9510 AVI
9440 BOR	9477 AVI	9511 AVI
9442 BOR	9478 AVI	9512 AVI
9443 BOR(Z)	9480 AVI	9513 AVI
9444 BOR	9481 AVI	9514 AVI
9445 BOR	9482 AVI	9515 AVI
9446 BOR	9483 AVI(Z)	9518 AVI
9447 BOR	9484 AVI	9520 AVI(Z)
9448 BOR	9485 AVI(Z)	9521 AVI
9449 BOR	9487 AVI	9522 AVI
9450 BOR	9489 AVI	9524 AVI
9451 BOR	9490 AVI	9526 AVI
9452 BOR	9491 AVI	9528 AVI
9453 BOR (Z)	9493 AVI	9529 AVI
9454 BOR (Z)	9494 AVI(Z)	9530 AVI
9455 BOR	9495 AVI	9532 AVI(Z)
9456 BOR	9496 AVI	9533 AVI
9458 BOR	9497 AVI	9534 AVI
9459 AVI	9498 AVI	9535 AVI

BB 12000 CLASS   Bo-Bo

Built: 1951-64 by Siemens/Alsthom.
Supply System: 25 kV ac overhead.
Continuous rating: 2470 kW (3310 hp).
Weight: 82-86 tonnes.
Length: 15.20 m (49 ft 11 in).
Maximum Speed: 120 km/h (75 mph).

12002 LEN	12006 LEN	12010 MOH
12003 MOH	12007 MOH	12011 MOH
12004 MOH	12008 THI	12012 LEN
12005 MOH	12009 MOH	12013 MOH

Top: SNCF BB 9200 class no. BB 9236 arrives at Béziers with the 0641 Bordeaux-Marseilles working on 05.07.87. *(D. J. Glossop)*

Bottom: SNCF BB 9300 class no. BB 9327 at Paris Sud Ouest Depot on 21.02.88. *(R. G. Morris)*

12014 MOH	12059 MOH	12107 THI
12015 LEN	12060 MOH	12108 LEN
12016 MOH	12061 MOH	12109 THI
12017 MOH	12062 MOH	12110 THI
12018 MOH	12063 MOH	12111 THI
12019 LEN	12064 MOH	12112 LEN
12020 MOH	12065 LEN	12113 MOH
12021 THI	12067 MOH	12114 MOH
12022 LEN	12068 MOH	12115 LEN
12023 LEN	12069 MOH	12116 MOH
12024 LEN	12070 MOH	12117 MOH
12025 MOH	12071 MOH	12118 MOH
12026 LEN	12073 LEN	12119 MOH
12027 LEN	12074 MOH	12120 LEN(Z)
12028 LEN	12075 MOH	12121 MOH
12020 MOH	12076 LEN	12122 THI
12030 MOH	12077 MOH	12123 MOH
12031 LEN	12078 THI	12124 MOH
12032 LEN	12080 MOH	12125 MOH
12033 MOH	12081 LEN	12126 LEN
12034 MOH	12082 MOH	12127 LEN
12035 LEN	12083 MOH	12128 LEN
12036 MOH	12084 LEN	12129 LEN
12037 MOH	12085 LEN	12130 LEN
12038 MOH	12086 LEN	12131 LEN
12039 MOH	12087 MOH	12132 MOH
12040 MOH	12088 MOH	12133 LEN
12041 LEN	12090 MOH	12134 THI
12042 MOH	12091 MOH	12136 THI
12043 LEN	12092 MOH	12137 LEN
12044 LEN	12094 MOH	12138 LEN
12045 MOH	12095 LEN	12139 LEN
12046 MOH	12096 MOH	12140 THI
12047 MOH	12097 MOH	12141 THI
12048 LEN	12098 MOH	12142 LEN
12049 MOH	12099 MPH	12143 LCN
12050 MOH	12100 THI	12144 THI
12051 MOH	12101 LEN	12145 THI
12053 LEN	12103 THI	12146 LEN
12054 MOH	12104 LEN	12147 THI
12055 MOH	12105 LEN	12148 LEN
12056 LEN	12106 THI	

BB 13000 CLASS   Bo-Bo

Built: 1954-57 by MTE/Fives-Lille/SLM/Jeumont/Oerlikon/BBC/Séchéron.
Supply System: 25 kV ac overhead.
Continuous rating: 2130 kW (2855 hp)[* 2000 kW (2680 hp)].
Weight: 84 tonnes.
Length: 15.20 m (49 ft 11 in).
Maximum Speed: 120 km/h (75 mph)[105 km/h (65 mph).

13003* STR	13024 STR	13044 STR
13005* STR	13027 STR	13045 STR
13006* STR	13029 STR	13046 STR
13008* STR	13031 STR	13047 STR(Z)
13009* STR	13034 STR	13050 STR
13011* STR	13038 STR	13051 STR
13017 STR	13039 STR	13052 STR
13020 STR	13041 STR	13053 STR
13023 STR	13043 STR	

BB 14100 CLASS   Co-Co

Built: 1954-58 by Alsthom/Fives-Lille/CEM.
Supply System: 25 kV ac overhead.
Continuous rating: 1860 kW (2495 hp).
Weight: 127 tonnes.
Length: 18.89 m (62 ft).
Maximum Speed: 60 km/h (37 mph).

14101 THI	14133 THI(Z)	14167 MOH
14102 THI	14146 THI	14169 MOH
14104 THI	14148 THI	14174 THI
14109 MOH	14151 THI	14181 THI
14113 MOH	14152 THI	14182 THI
14116 MOH	14153 THI	14183 THI
14123 THI(Z)	14154 THI	14187 THI
14124 MOH	14155 THI	14188 THI
14125 MOH	14156 MOH	14195 THI
14126 THI	14161 MOH	14200 THI
14129 THI	14162 MOH	14201 THI
14131 THI		

BB 15000 CLASS   B-B

Built: 1971-78 by Alsthom/MTE.
Supply System: 25 kV ac overhead.
Continuous rating: 4360 kW (5485 hp).
Weight: 87-90 tonnes.
Length: 17.48 m (57 ft 4 in).
Maximum Speed: 160 km/h (100 mph).
Note: 15055 was formerly test locomotive 10004 respectively. 15007 is currently test locomotive 10003, but is expected to revert to 15007 shortly.

15001 STR	Gretz-Armainvilliers	15034 STR	Sète
15002 STR	Longwy	15035 STR	Nogent-sur-Marne
15003 STR	Sarreguemines	15036 STR	Le Perreux-sur-Marne
15004 STR	Sedan	15037 STR	La Ferté-sous-Jouarre
15005 STR	Saint-Louis	15038 STR	Ars-sur-Moselle
15006 STR	Metz	15039 STR	Rosny-sous-bois
15007 STR		15040 STR	Livry-Gargan
15008 STR	Nancy	15041 STR	Sainte-Menemould
15009 STR	Reims	15042 STR	
15010 STR	Strasbourg	15043 STR	Maizières-les-Metz
15012 STR	Châlons-sur-Marne	15044 STR	Suippes
15013 STR	Longuyon	15045 STR	Raon L'Etape
15014 STR	Thionville	15046 STR	
15015 STR	Biarritz	15047 STR	Chelles
15016 STR	Charleville-Mézières	15048 STR	Hagenau
15017 STR	Saint-Avold	15049 STR	
15018 STR	Bondy	15050 STR	Vitry-Le-François
15019 STR	Montigny-Les-Metz	15051 STR	Aulnoye-Aymeries
15020 STR	Pau	15052 STR	Cambrai
15021 STR	Château-Thierry	15053 STR	Trouville
15022 STR	Pantin	15054 STR	
15023 STR	Meaux	15055 STR	
15024 STR	Lunéville	15056 STR	Vannes
15025 STR	Toul	15057 STR	
15026 STR	Epernay	15058 STR	Épinal
15027 STR	Creutzwald	15059 STR	Tourcoing
15028 STR	Villiers-Le-Bel	15060 STR	Creil
15029 STR	Aurillac	15061 STR	Sarrebourg
15030 STR	Forbach	15062 STR	Montmédy
15031 STR	Moyeuvre-Grande	15063 STR	Verdun
15032 STR	Chambly	15064 STR	Saverne
15033 STR	Gagny	15065 STR	Vaires-sur-Marne

BB 16000 CLASS   Bo-Bo

Built: 1958-63 by MTE.
Supply System: 25 kV ac overhead.
Continuous rating: 4130 kW (5540 hp).
Weight: 88 tonnes.
Length: 16.20 m (53 ft 2 in).
Maximum Speed: 160 km/h (100 mph).

16001 PLC Neuilly-sur-Marne		
16002 PLC	16004 PLC	16006 PLC
16003 PLC	16005 PLC	

16007 PLC Mantes-La-Jolie	
16008 PLC Drancy	

16009 PLC	16027 PLC	16045 PLC(Z)
16010 PLC	16028 PLC	16046 PLC
16011 PLC	16029 PLC	16047 PLC
16012 PLC	16030 PLC	16048 PLC
16013 PLC	16031 PLC	16049 PLC
16014 PLC	16032 PLC	16050 PLC
16015 PLC	16033 PLC	16051 PLC
16016 PLC	16034 PLC	16052 PLC
16017 PLC	16035 PLC	16053 PLC
16018 PLC	16036 PLC	16054 PLC
16019 PLC	16037 PLC	16055 PLC
16020 PLC	16039 PLC	16056 PLC
16021 PLC	16040 PLC	16057 PLC
16022 PLC	16041 PLC	16058 PLC
16023 PLC	16042 PLC	16059 PLC
16024 PLC	16043 PLC	16060 PLC
16026 PLC	16044 PLC	16061 PLC

16062 PLC   Dol-de-Bretagne

BB 16500 CLASS   B-B

Built: 1958-64 by Alsthom.
Supply System: 25 kV ac overhead.
Continuous rating: 2580 kW (3460 hp).
Weight: 71-74 tonnes (16700 weighs 81 tonnes).
Length: 14.40 m (47 ft 3 in) (16700 15.27 m (50 ft 1 in).
Maximum Speed: 90/140 km/h (56/87 mph).

16501 LEN	16546 LEN	16591 PLV
16502 LEN	16547 LEN	16592 PLV
16503 LEN	16548 LEN	16593 PLV
16504 LEN	16549 LEN	16594 PLV
16505 LEN	16550 LEN	16595 PLV
16506 LEN	16551 PLV	16596 PLV
16507 LEN	16552 PLV	16597 PLV
16508 LEN	16553 PLV	16598 PLV
16509 LEN	16554 PLV	16599 PLV
16510 LEN	16555 PLV	16600 PLV
16511 LEN	16556 PLV	16601 PLV
16512 LEN	16557 PLV	16602 PLV
16513 LEN	16558 PLV	16603 PLV
16514 LEN	16559 PLV	16604 PLV
16515 LEN	16560 PLV	16605 PLV
16516 LEN	16561 PLV	16606 PLV
16517 LEN	16562 PLV	16607 PLV
16518 LEN	16563 PLV	16608 PLV
16519 LEN	16564 PLV	16609 PLV
16520 LEN	16565 PLV	16610 PLV
16521 LEN	16566 PLV	16611 PLV
16522 LEN	16567 PLV	16612 PLV
16523 LEN	16568 PLV	16613 PLV
16524 LEN	16569 PLV	16614 PLV
16525 LEN	16570 PLV	16615 PLV
16526 LEN	16571 PLV	16616 PLV
16527 LEN	16572 PLV	16617 PLV
16528 LEN	16573 PLV.	16618 PLV
16529 LEN	16574 PLV	16619 PLV
16530 LEN	16575 PLV	16620 PLV
16531 LEN	16576 PLV	16621 PLV
16532 LEN	16577 PLV	16622 PLV
16533 LEN	16578 PLV	16623 PLV
16534 LEN	16579 PLV	16624 PLV
16535 LEN	16580 PLV	16625 PLV
16536 LEN	10501 PLV	16626 PLV
16537 LEN	16582 PLV	16627 PLV
16538 LEN	16583 PLV	16628 PLV
16539 LEN	16584 PLV	16629 PLV
16540 LEN	16585 PLV	16630 PLV
16541 LEN	16586 PLV	16631 PLV
16542 LEN	16587 PLV	16632 PLV
16543 LEN	16588 PLV	16633 PLV
16544 LEN	16589 PLV	16634 PLV
16545 LEN	16590 PLV	16635 PLV

Top: SNCF BB 12000 class no. BB 12066 runs light through Thionville on 06.07.87.
(D. J. Glossop)

Bottom: SNCF BB 13000 class no. 13045 at Pont à Mousson whilst working the
1226 Longwy-Nancy service on 06.07.87.   *(D. J. Glossop)*

16636 PLV	16681 PLV	16726 LEN
16637 PLV	16682 PLV	16727 LEN
16638 PLV	16683 PLV	16728 LEN
16639 PLV	16684 PLV	16729 LEN
16640 PLV	16685 PLV	16730 LEN
16641 PLV	16686 PLV	16731 LEN
16642 PLV	16687 PLV	16732 LEN
16643 PLV	16688 PLV	16733 LEN
16644 PLV	16689 PLV	16734 LEN
16645 PLV	16690 PLV	16735 LEN
16646 PLV	16691 PLV	16736 LEN
16647 PLV	16692 PLV	16737 LEN
16648 PLV	16693 PLV	16738 LEN
16649 PLV	16694 PLV	16739 LEN
16650 PLV	16695 PLV	16740 LEN
16651 PLV	16696 PLV	16741 LEN
16652 PLV	16697 PLV	16742 LEN
16653 PLV	16698 PLV	16743 LEN
16654 PLV	16699 PLV	16744 LEN
16655 PLV	16700 PLV	16745 LEN
16656 PLV	16701 PLV	16746 LEN
16657 PLV	16702 PLV	16747 LEN
16658 PLV	16703 PLV	16748 LEN
16659 PLV	16704 PLV	16749 LEN
16660 PLV	16705 PLV	16750 LEN
16661 PLV	16706 PLV	16751 LEN
16662 PLV	16707 PLV	16752 LEN
16663 PLV	16708 PLV	16753 LEN
16664 PLV	16709 PLV	16754 LEN
16665 PLV	16710 PLV	16755 LEN
16666 PLV	16711 PLV	16756 LEN
16667 PLV	16712 PLV	16757 LEN
16668 PLV	16713 PLV	16758 LEN
16669 PLV	16714 PLV	16759 LEN
16670 PLV	16715 PLV	16760 LEN
16671 PLV	10716 PLV	16761 LEN
16672 PLV	16717 PLV	16762 LEN
16673 PLV	16718 PLV	16763 LEN
16674 PLV	16719 PLV	16764 LEN
16675 PLV	16720 PLV	16765 LEN
16676 PLV	16721 PLV	16766 LEN
16677 PLV	16722 PLV	16767 LEN
16678 PLV	16723 PLV	16768 LEN
16679 PLV	16724 PLV	16769 LEN
16680 PLV	16725 LEN	16770 LEN

16771 LEN	16779 LEN	16787 LEN
16772 LEN	16780 LEN	16788 LEN
16773 LEN	16781 LEN	16789 LEN
16774 LEN	16782 LEN	16790 LEN
16775 LEN	16783 LEN	16791 LEN
16776 LEN	16784 LEN	16792 LEN
16777 LEN	16785 LEN	16793 LEN
16778 LEN	16786 LEN	16794 LEN

BB 17000 CLASS   B-B

Built: 1965-68 by Alsthom.
Supply System: 25 kV ac overhead.
Continuous rating: 2940 kW (3940 hp).
Weight: 78 tonnes.
Length: 14.94 m (49 ft).
Maximum Speed: 90/140 km/h (56/87 mph).

17001 ACH	17015 ACH	17029 ACH
17002 ACH	17016 ACH	17030 ACH
17003 ACH	17017 ACH	17031 ACH
17004 ACH	17018 ACH	17032 ACH
17005 ACH	17019 ACH	17033 ACH
17006 ACH	17020 ACH	17034 ACH
17007 ACH	17021 ACH	17035 ACH
17008 ACH	17022 ACH	17036 ACH
17009 ACH	17023 ACH	17037 ACH
17010 ACH	17024 ACH	17038 ACH
17011 ACH	17025 ACH	17039 ACH
17012 ACH	17026 ACH	17040 ACH
17013 ACH	17027 ACH	17041 ACH
17014 ACH	17028 ACH	

17042 ACH Chaumont-en-Vexin		
17043 ACH	17046 ACH	17049 ACH
17044 ACH	17047 ACH	17050 ACH
17045 ACH	17048 ACH	

17051 ACH Cormeilles-en-Parisis		
17052 ACH	17056 ACH	17060 ACH
17053 ACH	17057 ACH	17061 ACH
17054 ACH	17058 ACH	17062 PLC
17055 ACH	17059 ACH	17063 PLC

17064 PLC	17078 PLC	17092 PLC
17065 PLC	17079 PLC	17093 PLC
17066 PLC	17080 PLC	17094 PLC
17067 PLC	17081 PLC	17095 PLC
17068 PLC	17082 PLC	17096 PLC
17069 PLC	17083 PLC	17097 PLC
17070 PLC	17084 PLC	17098 PLC
17071 PLC	17085 PLC	17099 PLC
17072 PLC	17086 PLC	17100 PLC
17073 PLC	17087 PLC	17101 PLC
17074 PLC	17088 PLC	17102 PLC
17075 PLC	17089 PLC	17103 PLC
17076 PLC	17090 PLC	17104 PLC
17077 PLC	17091 PLC	17105 PLC

BB 20011 CLASS   B-B

Built: 1976-86 by Alsthom/MTE.
Supply System: 1500 V dc/25 kV ac overhead (dual voltage).
Continuous rating:
Weight:
Length: 17.48 m (57 ft 4 in).
Maximum Speed: 200 km/h (125 mph).

20011 STR   20012 STR

BB 20200 CLASS   B-B

Built: 1970 by Alsthom.
Supply System: 25 kV ac 50 Hz/15 kV ac 16.67 Hz ac overhead (dual voltage).
Continuous rating: 1660 kw (2225 hp) on 25kV, 2940 kW (3940 hp) on 15 kV.
Weight: 80 tonnes.
Length: 14.94 m (49 ft).
Maximum Speed: 90 (56 mph) on 25 kV, 150 km/h (93 mph) on 15 kV.

20201 STR	20206 STR	20210 STR
20202 STR	20207 STR	20211 STR
20203 STR	20208 STR	20212 STR
20204 STR	20209 STR	20213 STR
20205 STR		

CC 21000 CLASS

C-C

Built: 1969 (*1974) by Alsthom/MTE.
Supply System: 1500 V dc/ 25 kV ac ac overhead (dual voltage).
Continuous rating: 5900 kW (7910 hp).
Weight: 124 (*128) tonnes.
Length: 20.19 m (66 ft 3 in).
Maximum Speed: 100/200 km/h (62/125 mph).

21001 DIJ	21003* DIJ	21004* DIJ
21002 DIJ		

BB 22200 CLASS

B-B

Built: 1976-86 by Alsthom/MTE.
Supply System: 1500 V dc/ 25 kV ac ac overhead (dual voltage).
Continuous rating: 4360 kW (5845 hp).
Weight: 89 tonnes.
Length: 17.48 m (57 ft 4 in).
Maximum Speed: 160(*200) km/h (100 (*125) mph).

22201 DIJ			
22202 DIJ	Oyonnax		
22203 DIJ		22208 DIJ	22213 DIJ
22204 DIJ		22209 DIJ	22214 DIJ
22205 DIJ		22210 DIJ	22215 DIJ
22206 DIJ		22211 DIJ	22216 DIJ
22207 DIJ		22212 DIJ	22217 DIJ

22218 DIJ	Fourmies		
22219 DIJ	Albertville		

22220 DIJ		22227 DIJ	22233 DIJ
22221 DIJ		22228 DIJ	22234 DIJ
22222 DIJ		22229 DIJ	22235 DIJ
22223 DIJ		22230 DIJ	22236 DIJ
22224 DIJ		22231 DIJ	22237 DIJ
22225 DIJ		22232 DIJ	22238 DIJ
22226 DIJ			

22239 DIJ	Lons Le Saunier		
22240 DIJ		22243 DIJ	22246 MAR
22241 DIJ		22244 DIJ	22247 MAR
22242 DIJ		22245 DIJ	22248 MAR

22249 MAR		22258 MAR		22267 MAR	
22250 MAR		22259 MAR		22268 MAR	
22251 MAR		22260 MAR		22269 MAR	
22252 MAR		22261 MAR		22270 MAR	
22253 MAR		22262 MAR		22271 MAR	
22254 MAR		22263 MAR		22272 MAR	
22255 MAR		22264 MAR		22273 MAR	
22256 MAR		22265 MAR		22274 MAR	
22257 MAR		22266 MAR		22275 MAR	
22276 MAR	Dijon			22277 MAR	Is-sur-Tille
22278* DIJ					
22280 MAR	Hazebrouck				
22281 MAR		22282 MAR		22283 MAR	
22284 MAR	Gevrey-Chambertin	22287 DIJ	St-Jean-de-Maurienne		
22285 MAR	Chantilly	22288 DIJ	Louhans		
22286 DIJ	Béthune				
22289 DIJ		22290 DIJ			
22291 DIJ	La Ferté-Alais				
22292 DIJ		22295 DIJ		22298 DIJ	
22293 DIJ		22296 DIJ		22299 DIJ	
22294 DIJ		22297 DIJ			
22300 DIJ	Chalon-sur-Saône	22302 DIJ	Rive-de-Gier		
22301 DIJ	Villeneuve-d'Ascq	22303 DIJ	Croix		
22304 DIJ					
22305 DIJ	St-Rambert-d'Albon				
22306 DIJ					
22307 DIJ	Le Teil	22308 DIJ	Gisors		
22309 DIJ		22310 DIJ			
22311 DIJ	Pierrefitte	22319 MAR	Sorgues-sur-Ouvèze		
22312 MAR	Antibes Juan-Les-Pains	22320 MAR	Istres		
22313 MAR	Digne-Les-Bains	22321 MAR	Belleville		
22314 MAR	Tain l'Hermitage	22322 MAR	Bollène		
22315 MAR	Miramas	22323 MAR	Cagnes-sur-mer		
22316 MAR	Lomme	22324 MAR	Lannion		
22317 MAR	La-Tour-du-Pin	22325 MAR	Champigny-sur-Marne		
22318 MAR	Carpentras	22326 MAR			

22327 MAR	22328 MAR	

22329 MAR Quimper		
22330 MAR	22334 MAR	22337 MAR
22331 MAR	22335 MAR	22338 MAR
22332 MAR	22336 MAR	22339 MAR
22333 MAR		

22340 MAR Cavaillon	
22341 MAR	
22342 MAR Carnoules	
22343 MAR	22344 MAR
22345 MAR	

22346 MAR Aubagne	
22347 MAR	
22348 MAR Saint-Martin-de-Crau	
22349 MAR	22350 MAR

22351* REN Valognes	22354* REN Ancenis
22352* REN Sablé-sur-Sarthe	22355* REN Sevres
22353* REN Plaisir	22356* REN Lorient

22357* REN	22360 REN	22363 REN
22358 REN	22361 REN	22364 REN
22359 REN	22362 REN	22365 REN

22366 REN Malakoff		
22367 REN	22368 REN	22369 REN

22370 REN	Thouars	22386 DIJ	Bailleul
22371 REN	Ladoix-Serrigny	22387 DIJ	Liévin
22372 REN	Mauriac	22388 DIJ	Somain
22373 REN	Aulnay-sous-Bois	22389 DIJ	Cemines
22374 REN	Noyon	22390 DIJ	Lesquin
22375 REN	Méricourt	22391 DIJ	Hirson
22376 REN	Douai	22392 DIJ	Charles Tellier
22377 DIJ	Roubaix	22393 DIJ	Pont-á-Vendin
22378 REN	Le Quesnoy	22394 DIJ	Joinville-Le-Pont
22381 REN	Le Bourget	22395 DIJ	Nevilly-Plaisance
22382 REN	Clermont de l'Oise	22396 DIJ	Baie-de-Somme
22383 DIJ	Bully-Les-Mines	22397 DIJ	Pagny-sur-Meuse
22384 DIJ	Saint-André lez Lille	22398 DIJ	Coudekerque Branche
22385 DIJ	Longueau	22399 DIJ	

| 22400 DlJ | 22401 DlJ | 22402 DlJ |
| 22403 DlJ | 22404 DlJ | 22405 DlJ |

BB 25100 CLASS   Bo-Bo

Built: 1964-65 by MTE.
Supply System: 1500 V dc/ 25 kV ac ac overhead (dual voltage).
Continuous rating: 3400 kW (4560 hp) on 1500 V, 4130 (5540 hp) on 25 kV.
Weight: 85 tonnes.
Length: 16.20 m (53 ft 2 in).
Maximum Speed: 130 km/h (81 mph).

25101 CLY	25110 CLY	25118 CLY
25102 CLY	25111 CLY	25119 CLY
25103 CLY	25112 CLY	25120 CLY
25104 CLY	25113 CLY	25121 CLY
25105 CLY	25114 CLY	25122 CLY
25106 CLY	25115 CLY	25123 CLY
25107 CLY	25116 CLY	25124 CLY
25108 CLY	25117 CLY	25125 CLY
25109 CLY		

BB 25150 CLASS   Bo-Bo

Built: 1967-69 (*1974; + 1976-77) by MTE.
Supply System: 1500 V dc/ 25 kV ac ac overhead (dual voltage).
Continuous rating: 3400 kW (4550 hp)[1500 V]; 4130 (5530 hp)[25 Kv].
Weight: 85 (*+89) tonnes.
Length: 16.20 m (53 ft 2 in); * 16.68 m (54 ft 9 in); + 16.73 m (54 ft 11 in).
Maximum Speed: 130 km/h (81 mph).

25150 CLY	25159 CLY	25167 CLY
25151 CLY	25160 CLY	25168 CLY
25152 CLY	25161 CLY	25169 CLY
25153 CLY	25162 CLY	25170 CBY
25154 CLY	25163 CLY	25171* CBY
25155 CLY	25164 CLY	25172* CBY
25156 CLY	25165 CLY	25173* CBY
25157 CLY	25166 CLY	25174* CBY
25158 CLY		

Top: SNCF BB 15000 class no. BB 15058 at Strasbourg on 06.07.87.
(D. J. Glossop)

Bottom: SNCF BB 16000 class no. BB 16051 at Geneve. *(D. W. Fickes)*

25175* CBY Le Creusot		
25176+ CBY	25183+ CBY	25190+ CBY
25177+ CBY	25184+ CBY	25191+ CBY
25178+ CBY	25185+ CBY	25192+ CBY
25179+ CBY(Z)	25186+ CBY	25193+ CBY
25180+ CBY	25187+ CBY	25194+ CBY
25181+ CBY	25188+ CBY	25195+ CBY
25182+ CBY	25189+ CBY	

BB 25200 CLASS   Bo-Bo

Built: 1965-67 (*1974) by MTE.
Supply System: 1500 V dc/25 kV ac ac overhead (dual voltage).
Continuous rating: 3400 kW (4560 hp) on 1500 V, 4130 kW (5530 hp) on 25 kV.
Weight: 85 (*89) tonnes.
Length: 16.20 m (53 ft 2 in); * 16.68 m (54 ft 9 in).
Maximum Speed: 160 km/h (100 mph).

25201 REN Le Mans		
25202 REN	25217 REN	25232 REN
25203 REN	25218 REN	25233 REN
25204 REN	25219 REN	25234 REN
25205 REN	25220 REN	25235 REN
25206 REN	25221 REN	25236 CBY
25207 REN	25222 REN	25237 CBY
25208 REN	25223 REN	25238 CBY
25209 REN	25224 REN	25239 CBY
25210 REN	25225 REN	25240 CBY
25211 REN	25226 REN	25241 CBY
25212 REN	25227 REN	25242 CBY
25213 REN	25228 REN	25243 CBY
25214 REN	25229 REN	25244 CBY
25215 REN	25230 REN	25245 CBY
25216 REN	25231 REN	25246 REN

25247* REN Combourg
25248* REN
25249* REN
25250* REN Vitré
25251* REN Versailles

BB 25500 CLASS   B-B

Built: 1964-76 by Alsthom.
Supply System: 1500 V dc/25 kV ac ac overhead (dual voltage).
Continuous rating: 2940 kW (3940 hp).
Weight: 89 (*79, +77, #80) tonnes.
Length: 15.57 m (51 ft 1 in); *#14.49 m (47 ft 6 in); +14.70 m (48 ft 3 in).
Maximum Speed: 90/150 km/h (56/93 mph).

25501* LAB	25516* ACH	25530* ACH
25502* LAB	25517* ACH	25531* ACH
25503* LAB	25518* ACH	25532* LAB
25504* LAB	25519* ACH	25533* LAB
25505* LAB	25520* ACH	25534* LAB
25506* LAB	25521* ACH	25535* LAB
25507* LAB	25522* ACH	25536* LAB
25508* LAB	25523* ACH	25537* LAB
25509* LAB	25524* ACH	25538* LAB
25510* LAB	25525* ACH	25539* LAB
25511* LAB	25526* ACH	25540* LAB
25512* LAB	25527* ACH	25541* TSP
25513* LAB	25528* ACH	25542* TSP
25514* LAB	25529* ACH	25543* TSP
25515* LAB		

25544* TSP Parthenay		
25545+ TSP	25562# ACH	25579# ACH
25546+ TSP	25563# ACH	25580# ACH
25547+ TSP	25564# ACH	25581# ACH
25548+ TSP	25565# ACH	25582# ACH
25549+ TSP	25566# ACH	25583# ACH
25550+ TSP	25567# ACH	25584# ACH
25551+ TSP	25568# ACH	25585# ACH
25552+ TSP	25569# ACH	25586# ACH
25553+ TSP	25570# ACH	25587# ACH
25554+ TSP	25571# ACH	25588 ACH
25555+ TSP	25572# ACH	25589 ACH
25556# DIJ	25573# ACH	25590 ACH
25557# DIJ	25574# ACH	25591 ACH
25558# DIJ	25575# ACH	25592 ACH
25559# ACH	25576# ACH	25593 ACH
25560# ACH	25577# ACH	25594 ACH
25561# ACH	25578# ACH	25595 ACH

25596 ACH	25629 MAR	25662 ACH
25597 ACH	25630 MAR	25663 MAR
25598 ACH	25631 MAR	25664 DIJ
25599 ACH	25632 DIJ	25665 DIJ
25600 ACH	25633 MAR	25666 MAR
25601 ACH	25634 DIJ	25667 MAR
25602 ACH	25635 MAR	25668 MAR
25603 ACH	25636 MAR	25669 MAR
25604 ACH	25637 DIJ	25670 MAR
25605 ACH	25638 DIJ	25671 DIJ
25606 ACH	25639 DIJ	25672 DIJ
25607 ACH	25640 DIJ	25673 DIJ
25608 ACH	25641 DIJ	25674 DIJ
25609 ACH	25642 DIJ	25675 DIJ
25610 ACH	25643 DIJ	25676 DIJ
25611 ACH	25644 MAR	25677 DIJ
25612 MON	25645 MAR	25678 DIJ
25613 MON	25646 MAR	25679 DIJ
25614 MON	25647 MAR	25680 DIJ
25615 MON	25648 MAR	25681 DIJ
25616 MON	25649 DIJ	25682 DIJ
25617 MON	25650 DIJ	25683 DIJ
25618 MON	25651 MAR	25684 DIJ
25619 MON	25652 MAR	25685 DIJ
25620 MAR	25653 DIJ	25686 DIJ
25621 MAR	25654 DIJ	25687 DIJ
25622 MAR	25655 DIJ	25688 DIJ
25623 MAR	25656 ACH	25689 DIJ
25624 MAR	25657 ACH	25690 DIJ
25625 MAR	25658 MAR	25691 DIJ
25626 MAR	25659 ACH	25692 DIJ
25627 MAR	25660 ACH	25693 DIJ
25628 MAR	25661 ACH	25694 DIJ

BB 26000 CLASS   B-B

Built: 1988-90 by Alsthom.
Supply System: 1500 V dc/25 kV ac ac overhead (dual voltage).
Continuous rating: 5600 kW (7500 hp).
Weight: tonnes.
Length: m (ft in).
Maximum Speed: km/h (mph).

26001 DIJ	26003 DIJ	26005 DIJ
26002 DIJ	26004 DIJ	

26006 DIJ Musée Français du Chemin de Fer		
26007	26020	26033
26008	26021	26034
26009	26022	26035
26010	26023	26036
26011	26024	26037
26012	26025	26038
26013	26026	26039
26014	26027	26040
26015	26028	26041
26016	26029	26042
26017	26030	26043
26018	26031	26044
26019	26032	

CC 40100 CLASS   C-C

Built: 1964*/69-70 by Alsthom.
Supply System: 1500 V dc/3000 V dc/25 kV ac 50 Hz/15 kV ac 16.67 hz overhead (quad voltage).
Continuous rating: 5510 (*4480)kW (7380 (*6000) hp).
Weight: 109 tonnes.
Length: 22.03 m (72 ft 3 in).
Maximum Speed: 160 km/h (100 mph).

40101*	PLC	Perpignan
40102*	PLC	Menton
40103*	PLC	Brioude
40104*	PLC	Saint-Jean-de-Luz
40105	PLC	Hyères
40106	PLC	Compiègne
40107	PLC	Bayonne
40108	PLC	Hendaye
40109	PLC	Cannes
40110	PLC	Nice

MAIN LINE DIESEL LOCOMOTIVES

AIAAIA 62000 CLASS   A1A-A1A

Built: 1946-47 by Baldwin.
Engine: Baldwin 606NA of 560 kW (750 hp).
Transmission: Electric.
Weight: 110 tonnes.
Length: 17.70 m (58 ft 1 in).
Maximum   Speed: 96 km/h (60 mph).

62001 LEN	62030 LEN	62076 THI
62006 STR(Z)	62033 LEN	62078 LEN
62007 LEN	62038 LEN	62081 THI
62010 THI	62043 THI	62082 LEN
62011 LEN	62046 LEN	62083 THI
62012 LEN	62049 LEN	62084 THI
62014 STR(Z)	62051 LEN	62088 THI(Z)
62016 LEN	62057 STR	62089 STR
62018 THI	62061 LEN	62090 STR
62019 THI	62062 THI	62091 THI
62022 STR(Z)	62064 THI	62092 STR
62026 LEN	62065 STR	62094 LEN
62027 STR(Z)	62067 THI	62095 THI
62028 LEN	62071 THI	62099 THI
62029 LEN	62072 THI(Z)	

BB 63000 CLASS   Bo-Bo

Built: 1953-64 by B & L.
Engine: Sulzer 6LDA22B of 440 kW (580 hp); * Sulzer 6LDA22C of 440 kW
(580 hp); +Sulzer 6LDA22C of 535 kW (710 hp); Sulzer 6LDA22D of 535 kW
(710 hp); # Sulzer 6LDA22E of 550 kW (730 hp).
Transmission: Electric.
Weight: 64-69 tonnes.
Length: 14.68 m (48 ft 2 in).
Maximum Speed: 80 km/h (50 mph).

Top: SNCF BB 22200 class no. BB 22387 "Liévin" at Bobigny stabling point on 20.02.88. *(R. G. Morris)*

Bottom: SNCF BB 25150 class no. BB 25178 stabled at Aix Les Bains on 13.07.83. *(D. W. Fickes)*

63001 VSG	63046 MAR	63091* CBY
63002 VSG	63047 MAR	63092* DIJ
63003 TSP	63048 MAR	63093* PSO
63004 TSP	63049 MAR	63094* DIJ
63005 TSP	63050 MAR	63095* CBY
63006 TSP	63051 MAR	63096* DIJ
63007 TSP	63052 MAR	63097* DIJ
63008 TSP	63053 VSG	63098* DIJ
63009 TSP	63054 VSG	63099* DIJ
63010 TSP	63055 DIJ	63100* DIJ
63011 TSP	63056 VSG	63101* TSP
63012 TSP	63057 VSG	63102* DIJ
63013 TSP	63058 VSG	63103* NEV
63014 NEV	63059 VSG	63104* DIJ
63015 VSG	63060 PSO	63105* TSP
63016 MAR	63061 PSO	63106* TSP
63017 MAR	63062 NEV	63107* TSP
63018 MAR	63063 NEV	63108* PSO
63019 MAR	63064 NEV	63109+ CLY
63020 MAR	63065 NEV	63110+ NEV
63021 MAR	63066 MAR	63111+ CBY
63022 NEV	63067 NEV	63112+ LEN
63023 MAR	63068 VSG	63113+ PLV
63024 VSG	63069 MAR	63114+ NEV
63025 VSG	63070 MAR	63115+ NEV
63026 VSG	63071 MAR	63116+ LEN
63027 VSG	63072 NEV	63117+ CBY
63028 VSG	63073* DIJ	63118+ CBY
63029 VSG	63074* CBY	63119+ NEV
63030 VSG	63075* CBY	63120+ CLY
63031 VSG	63076* CBY	63121+ LEN
63032 VSG	63077* CBY	63122+ LEN
63033 NEV	63078* CBY	63123+ LEN
63034 VSG	63079* CBY	63124+ CLY
63035 TSP	63080* CBY	63125+ CBY
63036 TSP	63081* CBY	63126+ LFN
63037 PSO	63082* PSO	63127+ CBY
63038 TSP	63083* PSO	63128+ LEN
63039 MAR	63084* CBY	63129$ CLY
63040 NEV	63085* DIJ	63130$ VSG
63041 MAR	63086* DIJ	63131$PLV
63042 MAR	63087* PSO	63132$LEN
63043 MAR	63088* CBY	63133$LEN
63044 MAR	63089* CBY	63134$PLV
63045 MAR	63090* CBY	63135$PLV

63136$ PLV	63175$ LEN	63213# LEN
63137$ LEN	63176$ LEN	63214# PLV
63138$ LEN	63177$ PLV	63215# LEN
63139$ CLY	63178$LEN	63216# CLY
63140$ LEN	63179$ LEN	63217# CLY
63141$ LEN	63180$ PLV	63218# LEN
63142$ LEN	63181$ PLV	63219# LEN
63143$ LEN	63182$ LEN	63220# LEN
63144$ LAB	63183$ LEN	63221# CLY
63145$ LEN	63184$ LEN	63222# LAB
63146$ LEN	63185$LEN	63223# LEN
63147$ LAB	63186$LEN	63224# LEN
63148$ VSG	63187$LEN	63225# CLY
63149$ LEN	63188$LEN	63226# DIJ
63150$ LEN	63189$PLV	63227# DIJ
63151$ LAB	63190$PLV	63228# DIJ
63152$ LAB	63191$PLV	63229# CLY
63153$ LEN	63192$LEN	63230# LEN
63154$ LEN	63193$DIJ	63231# DIJ
63155$ LEN	63194$LEN	63232# DIJ
63156$ LAB	63195$PLV	63233# DIJ
63157$ LAB	63196# CLY	63234# LEN
63158$ LAB	63197# LEN	63235# PLV
63159$ PLV	63198# LEN	63236# DIJ
63160$ PLV	63199# LEN	63237# DIJ
63161$ PLV	63200# DIJ	63238# CLY
63162$ LEN	63201# PLV	63239# LEN
63163$ LEN	63202# CLY	63240# CLY
63164$ PLV	63203# LAB	63241# LEN
63165$ PLV	63204# LEN	63242# LAB
63166$ PLV	63205# DIJ	63243# LAB
63167$ LEN	63206# PLV	63244# LAB
63168$ LEN	63207# LEN	63245# LAB
63169$ LEN	63208# LAB	63246# LEN
63170$ PLV	63209# LEN	63247# LEN
63171$ PLV	63210# DIJ	63248# LAB
63172$ LEN	63211# CLY	63249# LAB
63173$ LEN	63212# PLV	63250# LAB
63174$ LEN		

BB 63400 CLASS

Bo-Bo

Built: 1959-60 by B & L.
Engine: MGO V12SH of 605 kW (810 hp).
Transmission: Electric.
Weight: 68 tonnes.
Length: 14.68 m (48 ft 2 in).
Maximum Speed: 80 km/h (50 mph).

63401 NAN	63409 NAN	63417 NAN
63402 SOT	63410 NAN	63418 LIM
63403 NAN	63411 ACH	63419 ACH
63404 SOT	63412 NAN	63420 NAN
63405 NAN	63413 NAN	63421 NAN
63406 NAN	63414 ACH	63422 ACH
63407 NAN	63415 ACH	63423 LIM
63408 BOR	63416 ACH	

BB 63500 CLASS

Bo-Bo

Built: 1956-71 by B & L.
Engine: MGO V12SH of 450 kW (605 hp).
Transmission: Electric.
Weight: 64-68 tonnes.
Length: 14.68 m (48 ft 2 in).
Maximum Speed: 80 km/h (50 mph).

63501 NAN	63513 AVI	63525 SOT
63502 ACH	63514 AVI	63526 CAN
63503 ACH	63515 VSG	63527 ACH
63504 BOR	63516 SOT	63528 STR
63505 SOT	63517 ACH	63529 SOT
63506 NAN	63518 ACH	63530 SOT
63507 SOT	63519 SOT	63531 ACH
63508 ACH	63520 ACH	63532 ACH
63509 REN	63521 REN	63533 ACH
63510 SOT	63522 SOT	63534 AVI
63511 SOT	63523 REN	63535 REN
63512 SOT	63524 SOT	63536 BOR

63537 ACH	63582 TOU	63627 VEN
63538 REN	63583 TOU	63628 NAN
63539 CAN	63584 AVI	63629 AVI
63540 TOU	63585 SOT	63630 SOT
63541 ACH	63586 BOR	63631 REN
63542 TOU	63587 STR	63632 LIM
63543 AVI	63588 PLV	63633 BOR
63544 AVI	63589 VEN	63634 VEN
63545 VEN	63590 ACH	63635 AVI
63546 ACH	63591 SOT	63636 PLV
63547 BOR	63592 STR	63637 NAN
63548 VEN	63593 BOR	63638 LON
63549 VEN	63594 BOR	63639 STR
63550 TOU	63595 TOU	63640 VSG
63551 BOR	63596 STR	63641 NAN
63552 LIM	63597 ACH	63642 MOH
63553 ACH	63598 CAN	63643 ACH
63554 AVI	63599 REN	63644 SOT
63555 REN	63600 BOR	63645 ACH
63556 SOT	63601 BOR	63646 STR
63557 TOU	63602 ACH	63647 REN
63558 ACH	63603 SOT	63648 NAN
63559 TOU	63604 NAN	63649 SOT
63560 TOU	63605 BOR	63650 CAN
63561 CAN	63606 ACH	63651 MOH
63562 REN	63607 STR	63652 ACH
63563 CAN	63608 STR	63653 SOT
63564 ACH	63609 BOR	63654 BOR
63565 TOU	63610 VEN	63655 MET
63566 ACH	63611 REN	63656 VEN
63567 ACH	63612 SOT	63657 AVI
63568 ACH	63613 SOT	63658 BOR
63569 TOU	63614 SOT	63659 AVI
63570 ACH	63615 SOT	63660 NAN
63571 CAN	63616 SOT	63661 MET
63572 NAN	63617 STR	63662 MET
63573 ACH	63618 STR	63663 REN
63574 ACH	63619 STR	63664 LEN
63575 MET	63620 NAN	63665 MOH
63576 ACH	63621 SOT	63666 MET
63577 TOU	63622 STR	63667 REN
63578 BOR	63623 SOT	63668 LON
63579 AVI(Z)	63624 AVI	63669 SOT
63580 TOU	63625 LON	63670 MOH
63581 SOT	63626 ACH	63671 AVI

63672 BOR	63717 MOH	63762 LEN
63673 LEN	63718 STR	63763 NAN
63674 SOT	63719 PLV	63764 NAN
63675 REN	63720 AVI	63765 BOR
63676 LON	63721 STR	63766 ACH
63677 LON	63722 STR	63767 NAN
63678 NAN	63723 STR	63768 NAN
63679 PLV	63724 LON	63769 NAN
63680 MOH	63725 STR	63770 NAN
63681 MET	63726 MET	63771 MET
63682 ACH	63727 STR	63772 LON
63683 BOR	63728 STR	63773 LON
63684 BOR	63729 LON	63774 PLV
63685 LON	63730 STR	63775 BOR
63686 PLV	63731 MET	63776 LON
63687 ACH	63732 LON	63777 LON
63688 VEN	63733 LON	63778 LON
63689 VEN	63734 LON	63779 VSG
63690 MOH	63735 LON	63780 VEN
63691 MOH	63736 MET	63781 MET
63692 VEN	63737 LON	63782 BOR
63693 VEN	63738 LON	63783 PLV
63694 VEN	63739 LON	63784 VSG
63695 MOH	63740 LON	63785 VEN
63696 MET	63741 MOH	63786 LIM
63697 VEN	63742 MET	63787 BOR
63698 REN	63743 PLV	63788 PLV
63699 AVI	63744 LON	63789 VEN
63700 MOH	63745 LON	63790 VEN
63701 STR	63746 MOH	63791 LON
63702 AVI	63747 PLV	63792 ACH
63703 LON	63748 MET	63793 STR
63704 LON	63749 MET	63794 ACH
63705 STR	63750 MET	63795 VEN
63706 LON	63751 LIM	63796 LON
63707 LON	63752 STR	63797 PLV
63708 MOH	63753 REN	63798 ACH
63709 PLV	63754 REN	63799 ACH
63710 AVI	63755 REN	63800 ACH
63711 PLV	63756 MET	63801 PLV
63712 ACH	63757 REN	63802 ACH
63713 STR	63758 REN	63803 ACH
63714 LON	63759 REN	63804 ACH
63715 AVI	63760 REN	63805 VSG
63716 MOH	63761 ACH	63806 PLV

63807 PLV	63852 MET	63897 NAN
63808 ACH	63853 VSG	63898 STR
63809 ACH	63854 VEN	63899 LON
63810 STR	63855 VSG	63900 AVI
63811 MET	63856 SOT	63901 AVI
63812 MET	63857 SOT	63902 PLV
63813 AVI	63858 MET	63903 SOT
63814 AVI	63859 VEN	63904 PLV
63815 PLV	63860 STR	63905 ACH
63816 MOH	63861 MET	63906 PLV
63817 AVI	63862 LIM	63907 REN
63818 VEN	63863 MOH	63908 NAN
63819 MET	63864 AVI	63909 STR
63820 MET	63865 VEN	63910 STR
63821 VEN	63866 LIM	63911 STR
63822 SOT	63867 MET	63912 STR
63823 MET	63868 MET	63913 MET
63824 MET	63869 LIM	63914 PLV
63825 AVI	63870 STR	63915 SOT
63826 PLV	63871 MET	63916 AVI
63827 MOH	63872 MET	63917 STR
63828 MET	63873 STR	63918 AVI
63829 STR	63874 STR	63919 MET
63830 AVI	63875 STR	63920 VEN
63831 AVI	63876 STR	63921 SOT
63832 VSG	63877 STR	63922 VEN
63833 MOH	63878 STR	63923 LON
63834 PLV	63879 STR	63924 LON
63835 MOH	63880 SOT	63925 MET
63836 LIM	63881 STR	63926 VEN
63837 AVI	63882 MET	63927 REN
63838 AVI	63883 STR	63928 VEN
63839 MOH	63884 STR	63929 LON
63840 MOH	63885 LON	63930 PLV
63841 STR	63886 PLV	63931 MET
63842 SOT	63887 PLV	63932 VEN
63843 MOH	63888 MET	63933 NAN
63844 MOH	63889 MET	63934 VEN
63845 MOH	63890 AVI	63935 LON
63846 AVI	63891 PLV	63936 LON
63847 MOH	63892 MET	63937 MET
63848 PLV	63893 MET	63938 PLV
63849 MOH	63894 PLV	63939 REN
63850 MET	63895 AVI	63940 VEN
63851 MET	63896 AVI	63941 NAN

63942 MET	63987 LIM	64032 LIM
63943 PLV	63988 LON	64033 MET
63944 BOR	63989 BOR	64034 SOT
63945 PLV	63990 LIM	64035 AVI
63946 VEN	63991 LON	64036 MET
63947 BOR	63992 VEN	64037 LIM
63948 BOR	63993 LIM	64038 AVI
63949 MOH	63994 SOT	64039 MET
63950 PLV	63995 LON	64040 LON
63951 AVI	63996 SOT	64041 SOT
63952 MET	63997 PLV	64042 SOT
63953 PLV	63998 PLV	64043 BOR
63954 PLV	63999 STR	64044 AVI
63955 LIM	64000 PLV	64045 MET
63956 LON	64001 BOR	64046 PLV
63957 LIM	64002 BOR	64047 REN
63958 TOU	64003 SOT	64048 REN
63959 MET	64004 BOR	64049 AVI
63960 LON	64005 BOR	64050 AVI
63961 NAN	64006 BOR	64051 MET
63962 LIM	64007 MET	64052 REN
63963 NAN	64008 MET	64053 AVI
63964 TOU	64009 SOT	64054 BOR
63965 ACH	64010 SOT	64055 PLV
63966 MOH	64011 LIM	64056 LIM
63967 NAN	64012 LIM	64057 VEN
63968 NAN	64013 LIM	64058 ACH
63969 AVI	64014 SOT	64059 SOT
63970 MET	64015 SOT	64060 MET
63971 VEN	64016 BOR	64061 MET
63972 AVI	64017 BOR	64062 MET
63973 MOH	64018 BOR	64063 PLV
63974 PLV	64019 SOT	64064 MET
63975 VEN	64020 SOT	64065 LON
63976 AVI	64021 LON	64066 LON
63977 MOH	64022 SOT	64067 LON
63978 AVI	64023 AVI	64068 LON
63979 STR	64024 AVI	64069 LON
63980 NAN	64025 SOT	64070 AVI
63981 BOR	64026 LIM	64071 AVI
63982 BOR	64027 LIM	64072 AVI
63983 LIM	64028 LON	64073 STR
63984 LON	64029 AVI(Z)	64074 STR
63985 BOR	64030 PLV	64075 AVI
63986 LIM	64031 SOT	64076 PLV

Top: SNCF BB 25500 class no. BB 25648 departs from Nice with the 1804 Cannes-Ventimiglia service on 05.07.89. *(D. J. Glossop)*

Bottom: SNCF BB 26000 class no. 26002 at Dijon Perrigny Depot on 28.11.88. *(D. Rowland)*

64077 PLV   64079 PLV   64080 PLV
64078 STR

BB 64700 CLASS   Bo-Bo

Built: 1956-71 by B & L.
Engine: MGO V12SH of 605 kW (810 hp).
Transmission: Electric.
Weight: 64-68 tonnes.
Length: 14.68 m (48 ft 2 in).
Maximum Speed: 80 km/h (50 mph).

64701 (6   )   64704 (6   )
64702 (6   )   64705 (6   )
64703 (6   )

BB 64800 CLASS   Bo-Bo

Built: 1953-64 by B & L.
Engine: Sulzer 6LDA22B of 440 kW (580 hp); * Sulzer 6LDA22C of 440 kW
(580 hp); +Sulzer 6LDA22C of 535 kW (710 hp); Sulzer 6LDA22D of 535 kW
(710 hp); # Sulzer 6LDA22E of 550 kW (730 hp).
Transmission: Electric.
Weight: 64-69 tonnes.
Length: 14.68 m (48 ft 2 in).
Maximum Speed: 80 km/h (50 mph).

64801 (63   )   64804 (63   )
64802 (63   )   64805 (63   )
64803 (63   )

CC 65500 CLASS   Co-Co

Built: 1955-59 by CAFL/CEM.
Engine: Sulzer 12LDA of 1470 kW (1960 hp).
Transmission: Electric.
Weight: 123 tonnes.
Length: 19.42 m (63 ft 9 in).
Maximum Speed: 75 km/h (47 mph).

65501 PLP	65517 PLP	65529 PLP
65502 PLP	65518 PLP	65530 PLP
65503 PLP	65519 PLP	65531 PLP
65506 PLP	65520 PLP	65532 PLP
65508 PLP	65521 PLP	65533 PLP
65513 PLP	65524 PLP	65534 PLP
65515 PLP	65527 PLP	65535 PLP
65516 PLP		

SNCF BB 63000 class no. BB 63159 at Paris La Vilette depot on 21.02.88.
(R. G. Morris)

BB 66000 CLASS   Bo-Bo

Built: 1960-68 by CAFL/CEM/Alsthom/Fives-Lille/SACM.
Engine: MGO V16BSHR of 830 kW (1115 hp).
Transmission: Electric.
Weight: 66-67 tonnes.
Length: 14.90 m (48 ft 11 in).
Maximum Speed: 120 km/h (75 mph).

66001 LEN	66047 TOU	66094 LON
66002 LAB	66048 TOU	66095 LON
66003 TOU	66049 NEV	66096 LON
66004 LAB	66050 TOU	66097 LIM
66005 LEN	66051 TOU	66099 LON
66006 TOU	66052 TOU	66100 LON
66007 VEN	66053 NEV	66101 LIM
66008 LAB	66054 LON	66103 LIM
66009 VEN	66055 TOU	66104 LIM
66011 TOU	66056 TOU	66105 LAB
66012 VEN	66057 NEV	66107 LIM
66013 VEN	66058 TOU	66108 NEV
66014 LAB	66059 NEV	66109 SOT
66015 LEN	66060 TOU	66110 LON
66016 VEN	66061 AVI	66111 NEV
66017 VEN	66062 TOU	66112 NEV
66018 LEN	66063 LON	66113 LON
66019 VEN	66064 TOU	66114 LON
66020 TOU	66065 AVI	66115 SOT
66021 LAB	66066 LON	66116 LON
66022 TOU	66067 LON	66117 NEV
66023 LEN	66068 AVI	66118 LON
66024 TOU	66069 NEV	66119 LAB
66025 AVI	66070 TOU	66120 NEV
66026 TOU	66071 TOU	66121 LAB
66027 LEN	66072 TOU	66122 LAB
66028 TOU	66073 NEV	66123 AVI
66029 AVI	66074 LON	66124 AVI
66030 LEN	66075 NAN	66125 SOT
66031 LEN	66076 NEV	66126 LON
66032 AVI	66077 NEV	66127 AVI
66033 TOU	66078 LON	66128 VEN
66034 LEN	66079 NEV	66129 LIM
66035 TOU	66082 LAB	66130 LIM
66036 TOU	66083 SOT	66131 TOU
66037 AVI	66084 TOU	66133 TOU
66038 VEN	66085 TOU	66135 NEV
66039 LAB	66086 TOU	66136 LIM
66040 AVI	66087 TOU	66137 NEV
66041 TOU	66088 LIM	66138 SOT
66042 LON	66089 STR	66140 SOT
66043 TOU	66090 LON	66141 TOU
66044 NEV	66091 LON	66142 LON
66045 LON	66092 LIM	66145 AVI
66046 TOU	66093 LIM	66147 NEV

66150 NEV	66203 NEV	66249 LON
66151 SOT	66204 NEV	66250 NEV
66153 SOT	66205 LIM	66251 CLY
66154 NEV	66206 AVI	66252 SOT
66155 NEV	66207 VEN	66253 LIM
66156 NAN	66208 SOT	66254 LIM
66157 NAN	66209 LAB	66255 VEN
66158 NAN	66210 AVI	66256 SOT
66159 NAN	66211 CLY	66257 LIM
66160 LON	66212 LON	66258 SOT
66161 NAN	66213 SOT	66259 NEV
66162 NAN	66214 VEN	66260 LIM
66163 NAN	66215 CLY	66261 LIM
66164 NAN	66216 LON	66262 LAB
66165 NAN	66217 CLY	66263 SOT
66166 NAN	66218 SOT	66264 SOT
66167 NAN	66219 NEV	66265 VEN
66169 NAN	66220 CLY	66266 VEN
66170 NAN	66221 LIM(Z)	66267 LON
66171 NAN	66222 AVI	66268 VEN
66173 NAN	66223 CLY	66269 LIM
66175 LON	66224 SOT	66270 LON
66179 SOT	66225 SOT	66271 LON
66180 SOT	66226 SOT	66272 TOU
66181 SOT	66227 CLY	66273 VEN
66182 SOT	66228 NEV	66274 LON
66183 SOT	66229 SOT	66275 LON
66184 NEV	66230 VEN	66276 LON
66185 NEV	66231 CLY	66277 LON
66186 SOT	66232 SOT	66278 CLY
66187 NEV	66233 VEN	66279 LIM
66189 VEN	66234 VEN	66280 LON
66190 LIM	66235 VEN	66281 LIM
66191 CLY	66236 VEN	66282 VEN
66192 LON	66237 VEN	66283 LIM
66193 LAB	66238 SOT	66284 LON
66194 LIM	66239 LIM	66285 SOT
66195 CLY	66240 LIM	66286 LIM
66196 LON	66241 LIM	66287 LAB
66197 VEN	66242 NEV	66288 LON
66198 AVI	66243 NEV	66289 LIM
66199 VEN	66244 NEV	66290 AVI
66200 LON	66245 NEV	66291 AVI
66201 NEV	66246 NEV	66292 CLY
66202 LIM	66248 NEV	66293 NEV

66294 SOT	66303 AVI	66311 TOU
66295 LAB	66304 LON	66312 SOT
66296 LON	66305 LON	66313 LIM
66297 AVI	66306 LIM	66314 LIM
66298 AVI	66307 LIM	66315 LIM
66299 AVI	66308 LON	66316 VEN
66300 LON	66309 LON	66317 TOU
66301 SOT	66310 LAB	66318 SOT
66302 LIM		

BB 66400 CLASS   Bo-Bo

Built: 1968-71 by CAFL/CEM/Alsthom/Fives-Lille/SACM.
Engine: MGO V16BSHR of 830 kW (1115 hp).
Transmission: Three Phase Electric.
Weight: 64 tonnes.
Length: 14.97 m (49 ft 1 in).
Maximum Speed: 120 km/h (75 mph).

66401 LEN	66425 CLY	66449 CLY
66402 LEN	66426 CLY	66450 LEN
66403 LEN	66427 CLY	66451 SOT
66404 LEN	66428 TOU	66452 SOT
66405 LEN	66429 LEN	66453 SOT
66406 LEN	66430 NAN	66454 SOT
66407 LEN	66431 CLY	66455 SOT
66408 LEN	66432 TOU	66456 SOT
66409 LEN	66433 LEN	66457 SOT
66410 LEN	66434 CLY	66458 SOT
66411 LEN	66435 NAN	66459 SOT
66412 CLY	66436 CLY	66460 SOT
66413 CLY	66437 CLY	66461 SOT
66414 CLY	66438 CLY	66462 SOT
66415 CLY	66439 NAN	66463 NEV
66416 CLY	66440 CLY	66404 NEV
66417 LEN	66441 CLY	66465 NEV
66418 TOU	66442 CLY	66466 NEV
66419 LEN	66443 CLY	66467 NEV
66420 CLY	66444 CLY	66468 NEV
66421 CLY	66445 LEN	66469 NEV
66422 CLY	66446 CLY	66470 NEV
66423 CLY	66447 CLY	66471 NEV
66424 CLY	66448 CLY	66472 NEV

Top: SNCF CC 65500 class no. CC 65527 stabled at Aix Les Bains on 13.07.83.
(D. W. Fickes)

Bottom: SNCF BB 66400 class no. BB 66451 at Sotteville Depot on 19.02.88.
(R. G. Morris)

66473 NEV	66485 LEN	66496 LEN
66474 NEV	66486 LEN	66497 NAN
66475 NEV	66487 LEN	66498 NAN
66476 LEN	66488 LEN	66499 TOU
66477 CLY	66489 LEN	66500 NAN
66478 CLY	66490 LEN	66501 NAN
66479 CLY	66491 LEN	66502 NAN
66480 LEN	66492 LEN	66503 LEN
66481 CLY	66493 LEN	66504 LEN
66482 NAN	66494 LEN	66505 LEN
66483 LEN	66495 LEN	66506 LEN
66484 LEN		

BB 66600 CLASS   Bo-Bo

Built: 1960-62 by CAFL/CEM/Alsthom/Fives-Lille.
Engine: SEMT 12PA4 of 890 kW (1195 hp).
Transmission: Electric.
Weight: 71 tonnes.
Length: 14.90 m (48 ft 11 in).
Maximum Speed: 120 km/h (75 mph).

66604 (66304) AVI(Z)	66611 (66311) AVI
66605 (66305) AVI(Z)	66612 (66312) AVI
66606 (66306) AVI	66614 (66098) AVI(Z)
66607 (66307) AVI	66615 (66102) AVI
66608 (66308) AVI	66616 (66106) AVI
66610 (66310) AVI	

BB 66700 CLASS   Co-Co

Built: 1985 onwards by CAFL/CEM/Alsthom/Fives-Lille/SACM.
Engine: MGO V16SHR of 830 kW (1115 hp).
Transmission: Electric.
Weight: 71 tonnes.
Length: 14.90 m (48 ft 11 in).
Maximum Speed: 90 km/h (56 mph).

66701 (66146) VEN	66711 (66188) VEN	
66702 (66080) VEN	66712 (66144) LEN	
66703 (66166) VEN	66713 (66139) LEN	
66704 (66174) VEN	66714 (66143) LEN	
66705 (66152) VEN	66715 (66081) STR	
66706 (66172) LEN	66716 (66177) LEN	
66707 (66176) LEN	66717 (66149) LEN	
66708 (66178) LEN	66718 (66)	
66709 (66148) LEN	66719 (66)	
66710 (66134) LEN	66720 (66)	

BB 67000 CLASS   B-B

Built: 1963-68 by B & L/MTE/SEMT.
Engine: SEMT 16PA4 of 1440 kW (1930 hp).
Transmission: Electric.
Weight: 80 tonnes.
Length: 17.09 m (56 ft 1 in).
Maximum Speed: 90 km/h (56 mph).

67001 CAN	67032 AVI	67069 NEV
67002 CAN	67033 AVI	67070 NEV
67003 CAN	67035 AVI	67071 NEV
67005 CAN	67038 AVI	67072 NEV
67009 NEV	67044 CAN	67073 NEV
67011 CAN	67045 CAN	67074 NEV
67012 CAN	67049 CAN	67076 NEV
67013 NEV	67050 CAN	67077 NEV
67014 CAN	67053 CAN	67079 NEV
67015 AVI	67055 CAN	67080 NEV
67016 CAN	67058 CAN	67081 NEV
67017 NEV	67060 CAN	67083 AVI
67019 AVI	67061 CAN	67084 NEV
67020 AVI	67062 CAN	67085 NEV
67022 CAN	67063 CAN	67086 NEV
67023 AVI	67064 AVI	67087 NEV
67024 AVI	67065 AVI	67088 NEV
67025 AVI	67066 AVI	67089 NEV
67026 AVI	67067 AVI	67090 NEV
67027 AVI	67068 NEV	67097 NEV
67031 AVI		

BB 67200 CLASS

B-B

Built: 1980-84 by B & L/MTE/SEMT.
Engine: SEMT 16PA4 of 1440 kW (1930 hp).
Transmission: Electric.
Weight: 80 tonnes.
Length: 17.09 m (56 ft 1 in).
Maximum Speed: 90/130 km/h (56/81 mph).

67201 (67006) NEV	67224 (67103) NEV
67202 (67011) NEV	67225 (67029) NEV
67203 (67040) NEV	67226 (67028) NEV
67204 (67034) NEV	67227 (67007) NEV
67205 (67037) NEV	67228 (67039) NEV
67206 (67030) NEV	67229 (67004) NEV
67207 (67021) NEV	67230 (67018) NEV
67208 (67008) NEV	67231 (67048) CAN
67209 (67118) NEV	67232 (67043) CAN
67210 (67120) NEV	67233 (67046) CAN
67211 (67108) NEV	67234 (67051) CAN
67212 (67122) NEV	67235 (67041) CAN
67213 (67115) NEV	67236 (67042) CAN
67214 (67123) NEV	67237 (67054) CAN
67215 (67102) NEV	67238 (67057) CAN
67216 (67121) NEV	67239 (67052) CAN
67217 (67117) NEV	67240 (67056) NEV
67218 (67112) NEV	67241 (67059) NEV
67219 (67091) NEV	67242 (67)
67220 (67114) NEV	67243 (67047) NEV
67221 (67081) NEV	67244 (67)
67222 (67078) NEV	67245 (67)
67223 (67082) NEV	67246 (67)

BB 67300 CLASS

B-B

Built: 1967-79 by B & L/MTE.
Engine: SEMT 16PA4 of 1525 kW (2045 hp).
Transmission: Three Phase Electric.
Weight: 80 tonnes.
Length: 17.09 m (56 ft 1 in).
Maximum Speed: 90/140 km/h (56/87 mph).

67301 CBY	67318 TSP	67333 CBY
67302 CBY	67319 TSP	67334 CBY
67303 TSP	67320 TSP	67335 CBY
67304 TSP	67321 TSP	67336 CBY
67305 NAN	67322 TSP	67337 CBY
67306 NAN	67323 TSP	67338 CBY
67307 CBY	67324 TSP	67339 CBY
67308 CBY	67325 CBY	67340 CBY
67309 TSP	67326 CBY	67341 NAN
67311 TSP	67327 CBY	67342 CBY
67312 TSP	67328 CBY	67343 CBY
67313 TSP	67329 CBY	67344 NAN
67314 TSP	67330 CBY	67345 NAN
67315 TSP	67331 CBY	67346 CBY
67316 TSP	67332 CBY	67347 CBY
67317 TSP		

67348 NAN	La Bernerie en Retz	
67349 NAN	67357 CBY	67364 CBY
67350 CBY	67358 CBY	67365 CBY
67351 NAN	67359 CBY	67366 CBY
67352 NAN	67360 CBY	67367 CBY
67353 CBY	67361 CBY	67368 CBY
67354 NAN	67362 CBY	67369 CBY
67355 CBY	67363 CBY	67370 CBY
67356 NAN		

67371 (67082) CAN		67381 (67111) CAN
67372 (67107) CAN		67382 (67101) CAN
67373 (67110) CAN		67383 (67119) CAN
67374 (67109) CAN		67384 (67099) CAN
67375 (67116) CAN	Draguignan	67385 (67105) CAN
67376 (67095) CAN		67386 (67094) CAN
67377 (67104) CAN		67387 (67124) NAN
67378 (67098) CAN		67388 (67096) NAN
67379 (67113) CAN		67389 (67093) NAN
67380 (67100) CAN		67390 (67291) NAN

BB 67400 CLASS

B-B

Built: 1969-75 by B & L/MTE.
Engine: SEMT 16PA4 of 1525 kW (2045 hp).
Transmission: Three Phase Electric.
Weight: 83 tonnes.
Length: 17.09 m (56 ft 1 in).
Maximum   Speed: 140 km/h (87 mph).

67401 NEV	67410 REN	67419 REN
67402 BOR	67411 CLY	67420 REN
67403 REN	67412 BOR(Z)	67421 REN
67404 REN	67413 CLY	67422 REN
67405 MAR	67414 LON	67423 CLY
67406 REN	67415 STR	67424 REN
67407 REN	67416 LON	67425 REN
67408 BOR	67417 REN	67426 REN
67409 CLY	67418 REN	67427 REN
67428 REN Dreux		
67429 BOR	67452 NEV	67475 REN
67430 REN	67453 NEV	67476 REN
67431 REN	67454 CAN	67477 REN
67432 REN	67455 NEV	67478 NEV
67433 CLY	67456 CLY	67479 NEV
67434 REN	67457 MAR	67480 BOR
67435 BOR	67458 NEV	67481 CAN
67436 BOR	67459 NEV	67482 MAR
67437 BOR	67460 NEV	67483 LON
67438 LON	67461 CAN	67484 MAR
67439 LON	67462 NEV	67485 LON
67440 CAN	67463 NEV	67486 LON
67441 CAN	67464 CLY	67488 MAR
67442 REN	67465 CAN	67489 MAR
67443 BOR	67466 CAN	67490 CAN
67444 NEV	67467 CAN	67491 CAN
67445 REN	67468 BOR	67492 CAN
67446 CAN	67469 NEV	67493 MAR
67447 CAN	67470 BOR	67494 MAR
67448 CAN	67471 BOR	67495 MAR
67449 NEV	67472 CAN	67496 MAR
67450 NEV	67473 BOR	67497 NIM
67451 CAN	67474 CAN	67498 STR

67499 STR	67510 STR	67520 STR
67500 REN	67511 STR	67521 STR
67501 NEV	67512 STR	67522 STR
67502 NEV	67513 STR	67523 STR
67503 NEV	67514 STR	67524 STR
67504 NEV	67515 STR	67525 NEV
67505 NEV	67516 STR	67526 CLY
67506 NEV	67517 STR	67527 CAN
67507 NEV	67518 STR	67528 NEV
67508 CAN	67519 STR	67529 CAN
67509 CAN		

67530 CLY Romilly-sur-Seine		
67531 NEV	67548 NEV	67564 NEV
67532 CAN	67549 MAR	67565 MAR
67533 CAN	67550 CAN	67566 NEV
67534 CAN	67551 CAN	67567 NEV
67535 NEV	67552 CAN	67568 MAR
67536 REN	67553 MAR	67569 STR
67537 REN	67554 NEV	67570 STR
67538 REN	67555 NEV	67571 STR
67539 REN	67556 NEV	67572 STR
67540 REN	67557 NEV	67573 NEV
67541 MAR	67558 NEV	67574 NEV
67542 NEV	67559 MAR	67575 MAR
67543 MAR	67560 MAR	67576 NEV
67544 CAN	67561 MAR	67577 NEV
67545 MAR	67562 NEV	67578 NEV
67546 NEV	67563 CAN	67579 NEV
67547 NEV		

67580 MAR Montpelier		
67581 NEV Nevers		
67582 CLY	67594 LON	67606 LON
67583 CLY	67595 LON	67607 LON
67584 CLY	67596 LON	67608 LON
67585 NEV	67597 LON	67609 LON
67586 STR	67598 LON	67610 LON
67587 STR	67599 LON	67611 LIM
67588 STR	67600 LON	67612 LIM
67589 LON	67601 LON	67613 LIM
67590 LON	67602 LON	67614 LIM
67591 LON	67603 STR	67615 LIM
67592 LON	67604 LON	67616 LIM
67593 LON	67605 LON	67617 LON

67618 LON		
67619 LON		
67620 LON Abbeville		
67621 LIM	67625 LIM	67629 LIM
67622 LIM	67626 LIM	67630 LIM
67623 LIM	67627 LIM	67631 LIM
67624 LIM	67628 LIM	67632 LIM

A1AA1A 68000 CLASS   A1A-A1A

Built: 1963-68 by CAFL/CEM/Fives-Lille.
Engine: Sulzer 12LVA24 of 1660 kW (2225 hp).
Transmission: Electric.
Weight: 104 tonnes.
Length: 17.92 m (58 ft 10 in).
Maximum Speed: 130 km/h (81 mph).

68001 NAN	68003 CLY	68004 CLY
68002 CLY		

68005 (68501) CLY

68006 NAN	68027 NAN	68049 TSP
68007 NAN	68029 NAN	68050 TSP
68008 TSP	68030 CLY	68051 TSP
68009 NAN	68031 CLY	68052 TSP
68010 TSP	68032 CLY	68053 TSP
68011 NAN	68033 NAN	68054 TSP
68012 NAN	68034 CLY	68055 TSP
68013 NAN	68035 NAN	68056 TSP
68014 NAN	68036 CLY	68057 TSP
68015 TSP	68037 CLY	68058 TSP
68016 CLY	68038 CLY	68059 TSP
68017 CLY	68039 CLY	68060 TSP
68018 NAN	68040 CLY	68061 CLY
68019 CLY	68041 CLY	68063 TSP
68020 TSP	68042 CLY	68064 TSP
68021 CLY	68043 NAN	68065 TSP
68022 CLY	68044 NAN	68066 TSP
68023 CLY	68045 CLY	68067 TSP
68024 CLY	68046 CLY	68068 TSP
68025 NAN	68047 CLY	68069 TSP
68026 CLY	68048 NAN	68070 TSP

Top: SNCF BB 67000 class no. 67005 at Sotteville Depot on 19.02.88.
(R. G. Morris)

Bottom: SNCF BB 67400 class no. 67515 at Strasbourg 20.09.89. (R. G. Morris)

68071 TSP	68075 TSP	68079 TSP
68072 TSP	68076 TSP	68080 TSP
68073 TSP	68077 TSP	68081 TSP
68074 TSP	68078 TSP	

68082 (68529) TSP	68084 (68508) CLY
68083 (68525) TSP	68085 (68510) CLY

A1AA1A 68500 CLASS   A1A-A1A

Built: 1964-68 by CAFL/CEM/SACM.
Engine: AGO 12DSHR of 1645 kW (2205 hp).
Transmission: Electric.
Weight: 102 tonnes.
Length: 17.92 m (58 ft 10 in).
Maximum Speed: 130 km/h (81 mph).

68502 CLY	68512 CLY	68520 CLY
68503 CLY	68513 CLY	68521 CLY
68504 CLY	68514 CLY	68522 CLY
68505 CLY	68515 CLY	68523 CLY
68506 CLY	68516 CLY	68524 CLY
68507 CLY	68517 CLY	68526 CLY
68509 CLY	68518 CLY	68527 CLY
68511 CLY	68519 CLY	68528 CLY

CC 72000 CLASS   C-C

Built: 1967-74 by Alsthom/SACM/SEMT.
Engine: AGO V16ESHR of 2250 kW (3020 hp). (72075 Pielstick 12PA6280 of 3530 kW (4720 hp)).
Transmission: Electric.
Weight: 114-118 tonnes.
Length: 20.19 m (66 ft 3 in).
Maximum Speed: 85/160 km/h (53/100 mph). (72075 85/140 km/h (53/87 mph)).

72001 CLY Annonay		
72002 CLY	72005 CLY	72008 VEN
72003 CLY	72006 VEN	72009 VEN
72004 CLY	72007 VEN	

72010 VEN   Bourg Argental

72011 VEN   72013 VEN   72014 REN
72012 VEN

72015 REN Paray-le-Monial
72016 REN   72018 REN   72020 REN
72017 REN   72019 REN   72021 VEN

72022 CLY Villemomble
72023 VEN
72024 REN Pont Audemer
72025 VEN
72026 CLY Luxeuil-Les-Bains
72027 CLY   72028 CLY   72029 CLY

72030 CLY Chalindrey
72031 CLY   72033 REN   72035 CLY
72032 REN   72034 CLY

72036 CLY Thann   72040 VEN
72037 REN   72041 CLY Chaumont
72038 CLY Nangis   72042 VEN
72039 CLY   72043 CLY Langres

72044 REN   72045 CLY   72047 CLY

72048 CLY Haute-Saône   72053 CLY Mautauban de Bretagne
72049 CLY   72054 VEN
72050 VEN La Palisse   72055 VEN
72051 CLY   72056 VEN La Bourboule
72052 REN La Baule

72057 REN   72058 VEN   72059 REN

72060 CLY Gray   72062 VEN
72061 VEN   72063 REN La Roche-sur-Yon

72064 VEN   72067 VEN   72069 REN
72065 REN   72068 CLY   72070 VEN
72066 REN

72071 CLY Marsaille   72076 CLY
72072 REN Saint-Malo   72077 CLY Noisy-Le-Sec
72073 REN   72078 CLY
72074 CLY Toulon   72079 CLY
72075 REN   72080 CLY Mulhouse

72081 REN		
72082 CLY	Provins	
72083 VEN	72086 CLY	72088 VEN
72084 VEN	72087 VEN	72089 VEN
72085 VEN		
72090 VEN	Belfort	
72091 VEN	72092 VEN	

DIESEL SHUNTING LOCOMOTIVES

Y 2200 CLASS B

Built: 1956-60 by Moyse/Decauville/Alsthom.
Engine: Poyaud 2BDT of 44 kW (59 hp); *Agron of 40 kW (53 hp).
Transmission: Mechanical.
Weight: 16 tonnes.
Length: 5.78 m (19 ft).
Maximum Speed: 50 km/h (31 mph).

Y 2203 STR	Y 2260 CBY	Y 2311 CBY
Y 2206 CLY	Y 2261 VEN	Y 2314 AVI
Y 2208 CLY	Y 2266 NEV	Y 2315 MAR
Y 2209 VEN	Y 2267 BEZ	Y 2316 AVI
Y 2210 CLY	Y 2272 ACH	Y 2317 VEN
Y 2215 CLY	Y 2280 LIM	Y 2319 LMS
Y 2219 STR	Y 2282 HEN	Y 2321* PLV
Y 2237 NEV	Y 2285 TAR	Y 2322* MET
Y 2240 DIJ	Y 2296 CAN	Y 2330* NAN
Y 2242 CBY	Y 2298 CBY	Y 2334* BEZ
Y 2243 CLY	Y 2301 MAR	Y 2336* AVI
Y 2247 CLY	Y 2306 SOT	Y 2337* MAR
Y 2255 BEZ	Y 2308 CBY	Y 2340* MAR
Y 2257 BEZ	Y 2309 AVI	
Y 2259 MAR	Y 2310 VEN	

Y 2400 CLASS B

Built: 1962-69 by Decauville.
Engine: Agron of 45 kW (60 hp).
Transmission: Mechanical.
Weight: 17 tonnes. **Length:** 7.18 m (23 ft 7 in).
Maximum Speed: 50 km/h (31 mph).

Y 2401 ACH	Y 2443 PSO	Y 2484 AVI
Y 2403 TOU	Y 2444 AVI	Y 2485 LIM
Y 2404 LIM	Y 2445 MAR	Y 2486 CAN
Y 2405 TAR	Y 2447 MAR	Y 2487 TSP
Y 2406 NEV	Y 2448 MAR	Y 2488 NEV
Y 2407 TOU	Y 2449 DIJ	Y 2490 REN
Y 2409 CLY	Y 2450 VEN	Y 2492 ACH
Y 2410 CLY	Y 2451 MAR	Y 2493 LIM
Y 2412 NEV	Y 2452 AVI	Y 2494 BOR
Y 2413 CBY	Y 2453 AVI	Y 2495 NEV
Y 2414 CBY	Y 2454 CBY	Y 2496 CLY
Y 2415 NEV	Y 2455 VEN	Y 2497 STR
Y 2416 LIM	Y 2456 MAR	Y 2498 STR
Y 2417 BEZ	Y 2459 MAR	Y 2499 CLY
Y 2418 LIM	Y 2460 VSG	Y 2500 MAR
Y 2419 LIM	Y 2461 DIJ	Y 2501 MAR
Y 2420 PSO	Y 2464 MAR	Y 2502 TSP
Y 2421 TOU	Y 2465 VSG	Y 2503 MAR
Y 2422 ACH	Y 2466 NEV	Y 2504 BEZ
Y 2423 BOR	Y 2467 CBY	Y 2505 REN
Y 2424 BEZ	Y 2468 BEZ	Y 2506 VSG
Y 2425 BEZ	Y 2469 BEZ	Y 2507 VSG
Y 2426 CBY	Y 2470 MAR	Y 2508 TAR
Y 2427 NEV	Y 2472 VSG	Y 2509 VEN
Y 2428 AVI	Y 2473 VEN	Y 2510 LIM
Y 2429 SOT	Y 2474 CBY	Y 2511 BEZ
Y 2431 SOT	Y 2475 VEN	Y 2512 CBY
Y 2433 PSO	Y 2476 CBY	Y 2513 VEN
Y 2435 NEV	Y 2477 NEV	Y 2514 NEV
Y 2436 TSP	Y 2478 DIJ	Y 2515 VEN
Y 2438 DIJ	Y 2479 DIJ	Y 2516 CBY
Y 2439 BEZ	Y 2480 NEV	Y 2517 CBY
Y 2440 VEN	Y 2481 ACH	Y 2518 NEV
Y 2441 DIJ	Y 2482 TOU	Y 2519 CBY
Y 2442 PLP	Y 2483 VSG	

Y 5100 CLASS   B

Built: 1960-63 by De Dietrich.
Engine: Poyaud 4PYT of 81 kW (107 hp).
Transmission: Hydraulic.
Weight: 17 tonnes.
Length: 7.18 m (23 ft 7 in).
Maximum Speed: 18 km/h (12 mph).

Y 5101 VEN	Y 5126 TOU	Y 5151 VSG
Y 5102 LMS	Y 5127 PSO	Y 5152 VSG
Y 5103 LMS	Y 5128 MET	Y 5154 LEN
Y 5104 NAN	Y 5129 MET	Y 5155 PLV
Y 5105 ACH	Y 5130 MOH	Y 5156 LEN
Y 5106 PSO	Y 5131 STR	Y 5157 LON
Y 5107 LAB	Y 5132 THI	Y 5159 THI
Y 5108 TOU	Y 5133 MOH	Y 5160 NAN
Y 5109 PSO	Y 5134 LEN	Y 5161 AVI
Y 5110 LIM	Y 5135 LEN	Y 5162 PLV
Y 5111 BEZ	Y 5136 TSP	Y 5201 ACH
Y 5112 MAR	Y 5137 CAN	Y 5202 LON
Y 5113 LEN	Y 5138 LMS	Y 5203 PLP
Y 5114 DIJ	Y 5139 LMS	Y 5204 TAR
Y 5115 VSG	Y 5140 VSG	Y 5205 LIM
Y 5116 NEV	Y 5141 VEN	Y 5207 VEN
Y 5117 LON	Y 5142 NEV	Y 5208 BEZ
Y 5118 LEN	Y 5143 PLV	Y 5209 STR
Y 5119 LON	Y 5144 LEN	Y 5210 STR
Y 5120 NAN	Y 5145 CLY	Y 5211 LON
Y 5121 SOT	Y 5146 DIJ	Y 5212 LEN
Y 5122 ACH	Y 5147 LON	Y 5213 TSP
Y 5123 BOR	Y 5148 LEN	Y 5214 PLP
Y 5124 LIM	Y 5149 LMS	Y 5215 LEN
Y 5125 LAB	Y 5150 LMS	

Y 6200 CLASS   B

Built: 1949-58 by Billard/Moyse.
Engine: Poyaud 6PDT of 132 kW (175 hp).
Transmission: Electric.
Weight: 30 tonnes.
Length: 8.90 m (29 ft 2 in).
Maximum   Speed: 60 km/h (37 mph).

Y 6201 MET	Y 6229 PSO	Y 6269 MAR
Y 6202 BOR	Y 6230 LEN	Y 6270 TOU
Y 6203 BOR	Y 6235 DIJ	Y 6271 TOU
Y 6205 MET	Y 6244 VSG	Y 6276 TOU
Y 6206 TOU	Y 6245 MAR	Y 6281 TSP
Y 6207 NEV	Y 6246 CLY	Y 6286 VSG
Y 6211 ACH	Y 6248 MAR	Y 6288 MET
Y 6213 DIJ	Y 6252 VSG	Y 6289 PLV
Y 6219 LAB	Y 6255 MAR	Y 6292 CLY

Top: SNCF A1A-A1A 68000 class no. 68084 at Paris La Plaine Depot on 21.02.88.
(R. G. Morris)

Bottom: SNCF Trakteurs Y 2306 & Y 6588 at Sotteville Depot on 19.02.88.
(R. G. Morris)

Y 6220 TSP	Y 6261 NEV	Y 6293 LMS
Y 6223 STR	Y 6262 MAR	Y 6297 CLY
Y 6225 PLP	Y 6264 MAR	
Y 6226 LON	Y 6267 MAR	

Y 6300 CLASS   B

Built: 1949-58 by Billard.
Engine: Poyaud 6PDT of 132 kW (175 hp).
Transmission: Electric.
Weight: 30 tonnes.
Length: 8.90 m (29 ft 2 in).
Maximum Speed: 60 km/h (37 mph).

Y 6302 NEV	Y 6314 NAN	Y 6322 CLY
Y 6303 CBY	Y 6315 NAN	Y 6323 MOH
Y 6304 VEN	Y 6316 NAN	Y 6324 DIJ
Y 6307 VSG	Y 6317 REN	Y 6327 CLY
Y 6308 NEV	Y 6318 NAN	Y 6329 STR
Y 6311 LEN	Y 6320 PLV	Y 6330 LEN
Y 6312 LEN	Y 6321 MET	

Y 6400 CLASS   B

Built: 1949-58 by De Dietrich/Decauville/SNCF.
Engine: Poyaud 6PDT of 132 kW (175 hp).
Transmission: Electric.
Weight: 30 tonnes.
Length: 8.90 m (29 ft 2 in).
Maximum Speed: 60 km/h (37 mph).

Y 6401 MET	Y 6414 NAN	Y 6426 VSG
Y 6404 PLP	Y 6416 ACH	Y 6428 VEN
Y 6405 MOH	Y 6417 BOR	Y 6429 VEN
Y 6407 CLY	Y 6418 DIJ	Y 6430 VEN
Y 6408 PLP	Y 6419 BOR	Y 6431 MOH
Y 6409 LON	Y 6421 CBY	Y 6432 MOH
Y 6410 LEN	Y 6422 VEN	Y 6433 CLY
Y 6411 CLY	Y 6423 VSG	Y 6435 MOH
Y 6412 MET	Y 6424 CBY	Y 6436 STR
Y 6413 ACH	Y 6425 CBY	Y 6437 VSG

Y 6438 PSO	Y 6495 CBY	Y 6550 SOT
Y 6439 BOR	Y 6496 REN	Y 6552 LEN
Y 6440 TOU	Y 6497 NEV	Y 6553 MET
Y 6441 BOR	Y 6498 CBY	Y 6554 BOR
Y 6442 TOU	Y 6499 TAR	Y 6555 REN
Y 6443 TOU	Y 6500 DIJ	Y 6556 LEN
Y 6444 TOU	Y 6501 MET	Y 6557 LON
Y 6445 TOU	Y 6502 MOH	Y 6559 LMS
Y 6446 TOU	Y 6503 CLY	Y 6560 LON
Y 6449 LAB	Y 6506 PLP	Y 6561 PLP
Y 6450 TOU	Y 6507 LEN	Y 6562 BOR
Y 6451 TSP	Y 6508 LEN	Y 6563 PLP
Y 6452 BOR	Y 6509 LON	Y 6564 CLY
Y 6454 CAN	Y 6510 THI	Y 6565 VSG
Y 6456 ACH	Y 6511 DIJ	Y 6566 MOH
Y 6457 REN	Y 6512 VEN	Y 6567 PLP
Y 6458 CAN	Y 6513 VSG	Y 6569 LEN
Y 6459 LMS	Y 6514 AVI	Y 6571 PLV
Y 6460 CAN	Y 6517 MAR	Y 6573 PLP
Y 6461 REN	Y 6518 MAR	Y 6574 CBY
Y 6463 ACH	Y 6519 MAR	Y 6575 PLP
Y 6464 NAN	Y 6520 MAR	Y 6576 BEZ
Y 6465 BOR	Y 6521 REN	Y 6577 BEZ
Y 6466 ACH	Y 6522 SOT	Y 6578 BOR
Y 6467 CAN	Y 6523 SOT	Y 6580 DIJ
Y 6468 VSG	Y 6524 VEN	Y 6581 PSO
Y 6472 MAR	Y 6525 CAN	Y 6582 TSP
Y 6473 BEZ	Y 6527 SOT	Y 6583 TOU
Y 6474 BEZ	Y 6528 SOT	Y 6585 SOT
Y 6475 BEZ	Y 6531 SOT	Y 6587 PSO
Y 6476 BEZ	Y 6532 NAN	Y 6588 SOT
Y 6477 BEZ	Y 6533 CAN	Y 6590 VEN
Y 6478 CLY	Y 6535 CAN	Y 6591 LAB
Y 6479 AVI	Y 6536 TOU	Y 6594 PLP
Y 6480 MAR	Y 6537 TSP	Y 6595 CAN
Y 6482 VEN	Y 6538 BOR	Y 6596 REN
Y 6483 VSG	Y 6539 TOU	Y 6600 LMS
Y 6485 DIJ	Y 6540 TAR	Y 6601 LMS
Y 6487 VEN	Y 6542 TSP	Y 6604 CAN
Y 6488 VEN	Y 6543 NEV	Y 6605 REN
Y 6489 AVI	Y 6545 TSP	Y 6606 PLP
Y 6490 DIJ	Y 6546 NAN	Y 6607 PSO
Y 6491 MAR	Y 6547 LMS	Y 6608 TSP
Y 6493 DIJ	Y 6548 LMS	Y 6609 LAB
Y 6494 VSG	Y 6549 REN	Y 6610 SOT

Y 6612 BOR	Y 6618 MAR	Y 6623 LEN
Y 6613 PSO	Y 6619 VSG	Y 6624 SOT
Y 6614 CLY	Y 6620 SOT	Y 6625 NAN
Y 6615 PSO	Y 6621 REN	Y 6626 LEN
Y 6616 VSG	Y 6622 REN	Y 6627 LON
Y 6617 LAB		

Y 7000 CLASS   B

Built: 1959 by Decauville/De Dietrich.
Engine: Poyaud 6PYT of 150 kW (200 hp).
Transmission: Mechanical.
Weight: 32 tonnes.
Length: 8.94 m (29 ft 4 in).
Maximum Speed: 60 km/h (37 mph).

Y 7001 ACH

Y 7100 CLASS   B

Built: 1958-62 by Billard/Decauville.
Engine: Poyaud 6PYT of 130 kW (175 hp).
Transmission: Hydraulic.
Weight: 32 tonnes.
Length: 8.94 m (29 ft 4 in).
Maximum Speed: 54 km/h (33 mph).

Y 7101 MOH	Y 7115 MOH	Y 7129 ACH
Y 7102 MOH	Y 7116 MOH	Y 7130 SOT
Y 7103 MET	Y 7117 MOH	Y 7131 BEZ
Y 7104 MET	Y 7118 SOT	Y 7132 MET
Y 7105 BEZ	Y 7119 MAR	Y 7133 MET
Y 7106 BEZ	Y 7120 BEZ	Y 7134 MET
Y 7107 LEN	Y 7121 BEZ	Y 7135 MET
Y 7108 PLP	Y 7122 LEN	Y 7136 MOH
Y 7109 SOT	Y 7123 LEN	Y 7137 MAR
Y 7110 SOT	Y 7124 LON	Y 7138 MAR
Y 7111 MOH	Y 7125 MET	Y 7139 BEZ
Y 7112 MET	Y 7126 LON	Y 7140 AVI
Y 7113 MOH	Y 7127 LEN	Y 7141 MAR
Y 7114 MOH	Y 7128 SOT	Y 7142 MAR

Y 7143 LIM	Y 7188 LEN	Y 7234 DIJ
Y 7144 MET	Y 7189 ACH	Y 7235 VEN
Y 7145 DIJ	Y 7190 MOH	Y 7236 LEN
Y 7146 LEN	Y 7191 LEN	Y 7237 LEN
Y 7147 LON	Y 7193 ACH	Y 7238 LEN
Y 7148 DIJ	Y 7194 MOH	Y 7239 TAR
Y 7149 SOT	Y 7195 MET	Y 7240 LIM
Y 7150 LON	Y 7196 MOH	Y 7241 HEN
Y 7151 NEV	Y 7197 VEN	Y 7242 BEZ
Y 7152 PLV	Y 7198 LON	Y 7243 AVI
Y 7153 TSP	Y 7199 PLP	Y 7244 AVI
Y 7154 TAR	Y 7200 MET	Y 7245 MET
Y 7155 BEZ	Y 7201 MOH	Y 7246 AVI
Y 7156 VEN	Y 7202 SOT	Y 7247 MET
Y 7157 BEZ	Y 7203 SOT	Y 7248 MOH
Y 7158 MET	Y 7204 MOH	Y 7249 VSG
Y 7159 NEV	Y 7205 MOH	Y 7250 DIJ
Y 7160 TSP	Y 7206 VSG	Y 7251 LON
Y 7161 LEN	Y 7207 LEN	Y 7252 LEN
Y 7162 ACH	Y 7208 BEZ	Y 7253 LON
Y 7163 TSP	Y 7209 BEZ	Y 7254 NEV
Y 7164 BOR	Y 7210 LON	Y 7255 HEN
Y 7165 ACH	Y 7211 PLP	Y 7256 NEV
Y 7166 DIJ	Y 7212 BOR	Y 7257 TSP
Y 7167 VEN	Y 7213 LIM	Y 7258 BEZ
Y 7168 TSP	Y 7214 NEV	Y 7259 MAR
Y 7169 HEN	Y 7215 VEN	Y 7260 MAR
Y 7170 SOT	Y 7216 LEN	Y 7261 MAR
Y 7171 BOR	Y 7217 LEN	Y 7262 MET
Y 7172 MET	Y 7218 SOT	Y 7263 MOH
Y 7173 BEZ	Y 7219 TSP	Y 7264 MET
Y 7174 LEN	Y 7220 LIM	Y 7265 HEN
Y 7175 BEZ	Y 7221 NEV	Y 7266 TSP
Y 7176 BEZ	Y 7222 NEV	Y 7267 LIM
Y 7177 MAR	Y 7223 NEV	Y 7268 BEZ
Y 7178 CAN	Y 7224 PLV	Y 7269 ACH
Y 7179 DIJ	Y 7225 LON	Y 7270 VEN
Y 7180 PSO	Y 7226 CAN	Y 7271 PLP
Y 7181 BEZ	Y 7227 ACH	Y 7272 LEN
Y 7182 MAR	Y 7228 MAR	Y 7273 VSG
Y 7183 LIM	Y 7229 AVI	Y 7274 LON
Y 7184 LEN	Y 7230 BEZ	Y 7275 MAR
Y 7185 ACH	Y 7231 MOH	Y 7276 VEN
Y 7186 HEN	Y 7232 MET	Y 7277 AVI
Y 7187 LIM	Y 7233 MET	Y 7278 VEN

Y 7279 CBY	Y 7290 MOH	Y 7301 CBY
Y 7280 VSG	Y 7291 MOH	Y 7302 VSG
Y 7281 SOT	Y 7292 SOT	Y 7303 AVI
Y 7282 SOT	Y 7293 ACH	Y 7304 MAR
Y 7283 LON	Y 7294 CAN	Y 7305 BEZ
Y 7284 PLP	Y 7295 ACH	Y 7306 BEZ
Y 7285 LEN	Y 7296 LEN	Y 7307 MAR
Y 7286 PLP	Y 7297 LEN	Y 7308 VSG
Y 7287 MAR	Y 7298 LON	Y 7309 DIJ
Y 7288 MAR	Y 7299 LON	Y 7310 VSG
Y 7289 VEN	Y 7300 VSG	

Y 7400 CLASS   B

Built: 1963-72 by Decauville/De Dietrich.
Engine: Poyaud 6PYT of 130 kW (175 hp).
Transmission: Mechanical.
Weight: 32 tonnes.
Length: 8.94 m (29 ft 4 in).
Maximum Speed: 60 km/h (37 mph).

Y 7401 PLV	Y 7423 VEN	Y 7445 PLP
Y 7402 PLP	Y 7424 AVI	Y 7446 CBY
Y 7403 PLV	Y 7425 MAR	Y 7447 REN
Y 7404 PLV	Y 7426 BEZ	Y 7448 NAN
Y 7405 PLV	Y 7427 BEZ	Y 7449 NAN
Y 7406 LON	Y 7428 AVI	Y 7450 REN
Y 7407 REN	Y 7429 BEZ	Y 7451 VEN
Y 7408 LEN	Y 7430 NEV	Y 7452 VEN
Y 7409 REN	Y 7431 MAR	Y 7453 VEN
Y 7410 REN	Y 7432 PLV	Y 7454 NEV
Y 7411 ACH	Y 7433 VSG	Y 7455 PLP
Y 7412 TSP	Y 7434 NEV	Y 7456 LON
Y 7413 BOR	Y 7435 DIJ	Y 7457 ACH
Y 7414 TOU	Y 7436 VSG	Y 7458 PLP
Y 7415 TSP	Y 7437 PLV	Y 7459 BEZ
Y 7416 TSP	Y 7438 PLV	Y 7460 BEZ
Y 7417 DIJ	Y 7439 LEN	Y 7461 VEN
Y 7418 DIJ	Y 7440 TSP	Y 7462 MAR
Y 7419 VSG	Y 7441 TSP	Y 7463 VEN
Y 7420 NEV	Y 7442 TSP	Y 7464 NEV
Y 7421 NEV	Y 7443 BOR	Y 7465 CBY
Y 7422 VSG	Y 7444 LEN	Y 7466 AVI

Y 7467 PLV	Y 7512 VEN	Y 7557 STR
Y 7468 REN	Y 7513 ACH	Y 7558 STR
Y 7469 VSG	Y 7514 LON	Y 7559 STR
Y 7470 ACH	Y 7515 LIM	Y 7560 TOU
Y 7471 PLV	Y 7516 ACH	Y 7561 TOU
Y 7472 VSG	Y 7517 ACH	Y 7562 VSG
Y 7473 LON	Y 7518 STR	Y 7563 VSG
Y 7474 PLP	Y 7519 SOT	Y 7564 STR
Y 7475 LIM	Y 7520 STR	Y 7565 STR
Y 7476 LIM	Y 7521 CLY	Y 7566 CLY
Y 7477 NEV	Y 7522 CLY	Y 7567 CLY
Y 7478 DIJ	Y 7523 CLY	Y 7568 REN
Y 7479 BEZ	Y 7524 CLY	Y 7569 NAN
Y 7480 AVI	Y 7525 LEN	Y 7570 NAN
Y 7481 REN	Y 7526 TOU	Y 7571 PLV
Y 7482 DIJ	Y 7527 TSP	Y 7572 VSG
Y 7483 LON	Y 7528 BOR	Y 7573 LIM
Y 7484 LEN	Y 7529 CBY	Y 7574 BOR
Y 7485 BOR	Y 7530 VSG	Y 7575 CBY
Y 7486 BOR	Y 7531 NEV	Y 7576 DIJ
Y 7487 NEV	Y 7532 BEZ	Y 7577 CLY
Y 7488 VSG	Y 7533 NEV	Y 7578 STR
Y 7489 BEZ	Y 7534 STR	Y 7579 STR
Y 7490 BEZ	Y 7535 STR	Y 7580 STR
Y 7491 STR	Y 7536 STR	Y 7581 SOT
Y 7492 PLV	Y 7537 STR	Y 7582 CAN
Y 7493 PSO	Y 7538 LEN	Y 7583 ACH
Y 7494 LON	Y 7539 PLP	Y 7584 CAN
Y 7495 BOR	Y 7540 REN	Y 7585 LON
Y 7496 NEV	Y 7541 TSP	Y 7586 LEN
Y 7497 DIJ	Y 7542 CBY	Y 7587 LEN
Y 7498 CBY	Y 7543 VEN	Y 7588 LEN
Y 7499 MAR	Y 7544 MAR	Y 7589 AVI
Y 7500 LEN	Y 7545 BEZ	Y 7590 BEZ
Y 7501 PLP	Y 7546 CLY	Y 7591 CBY
Y 7502 DIJ	Y 7547 CLY	Y 7592 BOR
Y 7503 CBY	Y 7548 STR	Y 7593 LIM
Y 7504 BEZ	Y 7549 PLV	Y 7594 TSP
Y 7505 BEZ	Y 7550 DIJ	Y 7595 ACH
Y 7506 PLP	Y 7551 TOU	Y 7596 DIJ
Y 7507 LEN	Y 7552 TSP	Y 7597 DIJ
Y 7508 BEZ	Y 7553 CBY	Y 7598 CBY
Y 7509 NEV	Y 7554 DIJ	Y 7599 CLY
Y 7510 LON	Y 7555 MAR	Y 7600 STR
Y 7511 LON	Y 7556 STR	Y 7601 REN

Y 7602 NAN	Y 7647 LIM	Y 7692 MAR
Y 7603 REN	Y 7648 TSP	Y 7693 VEN
Y 7604 LAB	Y 7649 PSO	Y 7694 BEZ
Y 7605 NAN	Y 7650 PSO	Y 7695 TSP
Y 7606 REN	Y 7651 TSP	Y 7696 TOU
Y 7607 PLP	Y 7652 CLY	Y 7697 TOU
Y 7608 LEN	Y 7653 NAN	Y 7698 LIM
Y 7609 VEN	Y 7654 VEN	Y 7699 LIM
Y 7610 VEN	Y 7655 LON	Y 7700 PSO
Y 7611 AVI	Y 7656 LON	Y 7701 NAN
Y 7612 BOR	Y 7657 PLP	Y 7702 REN
Y 7613 BOR	Y 7658 LEN	Y 7703 CLY
Y 7614 BOR	Y 7659 ACH	Y 7704 NEV
Y 7615 BOR	Y 7660 ACH	Y 7705 CAN
Y 7616 VSG	Y 7661 CAN	Y 7706 PSO
Y 7617 VSG	Y 7662 DIJ	Y 7707 STR
Y 7618 VSG	Y 7663 DIJ	Y 7708 CLY
Y 7619 NEV	Y 7664 LON	Y 7709 CLY
Y 7620 PLV	Y 7665 NEV	Y 7710 BOR
Y 7621 CLY	Y 7666 BEZ	Y 7711 TOU
Y 7622 ACH	Y 7667 MAR	Y 7712 LON
Y 7623 CLY	Y 7668 BEZ	Y 7713 ACH
Y 7624 STR	Y 7669 PLP	Y 7714 BOR
Y 7625 BOR	Y 7670 PSO	Y 7715 NAN
Y 7626 LIM	Y 7671 LAB	Y 7716 LAB
Y 7627 DIJ	Y 7672 BOR	Y 7717 TSP
Y 7628 PSO	Y 7673 BOR	Y 7718 TOU
Y 7629 PSO	Y 7674 PLV	Y 7719 CBY
Y 7630 PSO	Y 7675 CLY	Y 7720 VSG
Y 7631 LON	Y 7676 ACH	Y 7721 DIJ
Y 7632 BOR	Y 7677 PLP	Y 7722 VEN
Y 7633 CLY	Y 7678 PLP	Y 7723 BEZ
Y 7634 STR	Y 7679 PLP	Y 7724 AVI
Y 7635 LEN	Y 7680 REN	Y 7725 LIM
Y 7636 LEN	Y 7681 NAN	Y 7726 BOR
Y 7637 PLP	Y 7682 ACII	Y 7727 TOU
Y 7638 REN	Y 7683 BOR	Y 7728 BOR
Y 7639 ACH	Y 7684 LIM	Y 7729 STR
Y 7640 NEV	Y 7685 TOU	Y 7730 CLY
Y 7641 VSG	Y 7686 TSP	Y 7731 PLP
Y 7642 VEN	Y 7687 BOR	Y 7732 DIJ
Y 7643 NEV	Y 7688 NEV	Y 7733 PLP
Y 7644 VEN	Y 7689 VEN	Y 7734 REN
Y 7645 BEZ	Y 7690 VSG	Y 7735 REN
Y 7646 NEV	Y 7691 CBY	Y 7736 TOU

Top: SNCF Y 2400 class no. Y 2442 at Paris La Plaine Depot on 21.02.88.
(R. G. Morris)

Bottom: SNCF Y 5100 class no. Y 5159 at Thionville 28.09.89.   *(R. G. Morris)*

Y 7737 TOU	Y 7782 DIJ	Y 7827 BOR
Y 7738 TOU	Y 7783 CBY	Y 7828 HEN
Y 7739 VSG	Y 7784 AVI	Y 7829 TOU
Y 7740 CLY	Y 7785 VEN	Y 7830 VSG
Y 7741 NEV	Y 7786 MAR	Y 7831 NEV
Y 7742 BEZ	Y 7787 LIM	Y 7832 NEV
Y 7743 AVI	Y 7788 PSO	Y 7833 DIJ
Y 7744 TOU	Y 7789 LIM	Y 7834 CLY
Y 7745 LAB	Y 7790 TSP	Y 7835 CLY
Y 7746 LAB	Y 7791 BOR	Y 7836 LEN
Y 7747 BOR	Y 7792 TOU	Y 7837 DIJ
Y 7748 CLY	Y 7793 CLY	Y 7838 REN
Y 7749 STR	Y 7794 CLY	Y 7839 CAN
Y 7750 SOT	Y 7795 TSP	Y 7840 REN
Y 7751 LON	Y 7796 STR	Y 7841 REN
Y 7752 LON	Y 7797 STR	Y 7842 TOU
Y 7753 VSG	Y 7798 STR	Y 7843 TOU
Y 7754 REN	Y 7799 PLP	Y 7844 PSO
Y 7755 NAN	Y 7800 LEN	Y 7845 LIM
Y 7756 NAN	Y 7801 NAN	Y 7846 BOR
Y 7757 BOR	Y 7802 TOU	Y 7847 CBY
Y 7758 PSO	Y 7803 NAN	Y 7848 DIJ
Y 7759 PSO	Y 7804 BEZ	Y 7849 VSG
Y 7760 VEN	Y 7805 CBY	Y 7850 VSG
Y 7761 VSG	Y 7806 NEV	Y 7851 VEN
Y 7762 VEN	Y 7807 PSO	Y 7852 CLY
Y 7763 MAR	Y 7808 LAB	Y 7853 CLY
Y 7764 BEZ	Y 7809 TSP	Y 7854 PLP
Y 7765 VEN	Y 7810 LIM	Y 7855 CAN
Y 7766 NEV	Y 7811 STR	Y 7856 NAN
Y 7767 LIM	Y 7812 NAN	Y 7857 NAN
Y 7768 BOR	Y 7813 NAN	Y 7858 ACH
Y 7769 LON	Y 7814 REN	Y 7859 CAN
Y 7770 CLY	Y 7815 CLY	Y 7860 NEV
Y 7771 NAN	Y 7816 STR	Y 7861 CBY
Y 7772 LEN	Y 7817 CLY	Y 7862 VEN
Y 7773 DIJ	Y 7818 PLP	Y 7863 REN
Y 7774 LEN	Y 7819 LON	Y 7864 CAN
Y 7775 NAN	Y 7820 BEZ	Y 7865 SOT
Y 7776 NAN	Y 7821 STR	Y 7866 NAN
Y 7777 SOT	Y 7822 REN	Y 7867 LIM
Y 7778 LIM	Y 7823 REN	Y 7868 PSO
Y 7779 LIM	Y 7824 SOT	Y 7869 TSP
Y 7780 TAR	Y 7825 HEN	Y 7870 CAN
Y 7781 NEV	Y 7826 TSP	Y 7871 NAN

Y 7872 REN	Y 7878 NEV	Y 7884 DIJ
Y 7873 REN	Y 7879 REN	Y 7885 VEN
Y 7874 STR	Y 7880 REN	Y 7886 NEV
Y 7875 STR	Y 7881 CAN	Y 7887 CBY
Y 7876 STR	Y 7882 ACH	Y 7888 VEN
Y 7877 VSG	Y 7883 DIJ	

Y 8000 CLASS   B

Built: 1977 onwards by Moyse/Fauvet-Girel.
Engine: Poyaud Y12-520NS of 215 kW (290 hp).
Transmission: Hydraulic. Voith.
Weight: 36 tonnes.
Length: 10.14 m (33 ft 3 in).
Maximum   Speed: 60 km/h (37 mph).

Y 8001 TSP	Y 8028 LYV	Y 8055 LYV
Y 8002 MET	Y 8029 LYV	Y 8056 ACH
Y 8003 MET	Y 8030 REN	Y 8057 SOT
Y 8004 MET	Y 8031 REN	Y 8058 SOT
Y 8005 MET	Y 8032 REN	Y 8059 SOT
Y 8006 STR	Y 8033 REN	Y 8060 SOT
Y 8007 MET	Y 8034 NEV	Y 8061 MAR
Y 8008 MET	Y 8035 NEV	Y 8062 BEZ
Y 8009 MET	Y 8036 CBY	Y 8063 MAR
Y 8010 MET	Y 8037 CBY	Y 8064 DIJ
Y 8011 MET	Y 8038 ACH	Y 8065 MAR
Y 8012 MET	Y 8039 REN	Y 8066 DIJ
Y 8013 MET	Y 8040 NAN	Y 8067 TSP
Y 8014 STR	Y 8041 NAN	Y 8068 TSP
Y 8015 MET	Y 8042 MAR	Y 8069 TSP
Y 8016 MAR	Y 8043 MAR	Y 8070 LEN
Y 8017 MAR	Y 8044 MAR	Y 8071 LON
Y 8018 MAR	Y 8045 BEZ	Y 8072 BOR
Y 8019 MAR	Y 8046 DIJ	Y 8073 BOR
Y 8020 TSP	Y 8047 DIJ	Y 8074 LEN
Y 8021 DIJ	Y 8048 NAN	Y 8075 LEN
Y 8022 DIJ	Y 8049 ACH	Y 8076 TSP
Y 8023 REN	Y 8050 ACH	Y 8077 TSP
Y 8024 SOT	Y 8051 ACH	Y 8078 BOR
Y 8025 NAN	Y 8052 DIJ	Y 8079 LON
Y 8026 BEZ	Y 8053 DIJ	Y 8080 BOR
Y 8027 DIJ	Y 8054 LYV	Y 8081 TSP

Y 8082 LON	Y 8127 PLV	Y 8172 MAR
Y 8083 LON	Y 8128 PLV	Y 8173 MAR
Y 8084 TOU	Y 8129 PLV	Y 8174 BEZ
Y 8085 TOU	Y 8130 LIM	Y 8175 NEV
Y 8086 LON	Y 8131 TSP	Y 8176 LYV
Y 8087 LEN	Y 8132 TSP	Y 8177 NEV
Y 8088 LEN	Y 8133 TSP	Y 8178 MAR
Y 8089 LIM	Y 8134 MET	Y 8179 MAR
Y 8090 LIM	Y 8135 PLV	Y 8180 DIJ
Y 8091 LYV	Y 8136 MET	Y 8181 MET
Y 8092 PLP	Y 8137 MET	Y 8182 MET
Y 8093 LYV	Y 8138 BEZ	Y 8183 PLV
Y 8094 CBY	Y 8139 CBY	Y 8184 STR
Y 8095 NEV	Y 8140 NAN	Y 8185 STR
Y 8096 LYV	Y 8141 NEV	Y 8186 PLV
Y 8097 NAN	Y 8142 LYV	Y 8187 MET
Y 8098 NAN	Y 8143 REN	Y 8188 PLV
Y 8099 NAN	Y 8144 SOT	Y 8189 BOR
Y 8100 NAN	Y 8145 ACH	Y 8190 TSP
Y 8101 REN	Y 8146 ACH	Y 8191 TSP
Y 8102 ACH	Y 8147 MAR	Y 8192 TOU
Y 8103 BEZ	Y 8148 BEZ	Y 8193 PLV
Y 8104 MAR	Y 8149 PLV	Y 8194 BOR
Y 8105 BEZ	Y 8150 PLV	Y 8195 BOR
Y 8106 DIJ	Y 8151 PLV	Y 8196 BOR
Y 8107 REN	Y 8152 MET	Y 8197 TOU
Y 8108 MET	Y 8153 PLV	Y 8198 LIM
Y 8109 STR	Y 8154 PSO	Y 8199 TSP
Y 8110 MET	Y 8155 TSP	Y 8200 LEN
Y 8111 TOU	Y 8156 LIM	Y 8201 PLV
Y 8112 STR	Y 8157 LIM	Y 8202 PLV
Y 8113 LYV	Y 8158 TSP	Y 8203 SOT
Y 8114 CBY	Y 8159 TSP	Y 8204 NAN
Y 8115 PLV	Y 8160 REN	Y 8205 SOT
Y 8116 STR	Y 8161 NAN	Y 8206 NEV
Y 8117 STR	Y 8162 SOT	Y 8207 NEV
Y 8118 MET	Y 8163 ACH	Y 8208 BEZ
Y 8119 DIJ	Y 8164 SOT	Y 8209 CBY
Y 8120 CBY	Y 8165 SOT	Y 8210 MAR
Y 8121 NEV	Y 8166 TOU	Y 8211 MET
Y 8122 ACH	Y 8167 BOR	Y 8212 STR
Y 8123 MET	Y 8168 TOU	Y 8213 STR
Y 8124 MET	Y 8169 LEN	Y 8214 MET
Y 8125 MET	Y 8170 LEN	Y 8215 PLV
Y 8126 PLV	Y 8171 LEN	Y 8216 STR

Top: SNCF Y 7100 class no. Y 7120 at Béziers on 05.07.87.   *(D. J. Glossop)*

Bottom: SNCF Y 7400 class nos. Y 7553 & Y 7591 stabled at Aix Les Bains on 13.07.83.   *(D. W. Fickes)*

Y 8217 TSP	Y 8262 LEN	Y 8307 ACH
Y 8218 TSP	Y 8263 TSP	Y 8308 ACH
Y 8219 BOR	Y 8264 LIM	Y 8309 ACH
Y 8220 TOU	Y 8265 BOR	Y 8310 ACH
Y 8221 PLV	Y 8266 LEN	Y 8311 LIM
Y 8222 LEN	Y 8267 LEN	Y 8312 TOU
Y 8223 LON	Y 8268 LON	Y 8313 TSP
Y 8224 LON	Y 8269 TSP	Y 8314 TSP
Y 8225 SOT	Y 8270 LIM	Y 8315 TSP
Y 8226 NAN	Y 8271 TOU	Y 8316 TSP
Y 8227 REN	Y 8272 LIM	Y 8317 REN
Y 8228 NAN	Y 8273 NEV	Y 8318 TSP
Y 8229 ACH	Y 8274 NEV	Y 8319 ACH
Y 8230 ACH	Y 8275 PLV	Y 8320 TSP
Y 8231 NEV	Y 8276 PLP	Y 8321 NAN
Y 8232 CBY	Y 8277 MET	Y 8322 MET
Y 8233 BEZ	Y 8278 LEN	Y 8323 LEN
Y 8234 MAR	Y 8279 LEN	Y 8324 CBY
Y 8235 NEV	Y 8280 LEN	Y 8325 LIM
Y 8236 NEV	Y 8281 LEN	Y 8326 PLV
Y 8237 BEZ	Y 8282 PLV	Y 8327 MET
Y 8238 NEV	Y 8283 BEZ	Y 8328 LON
Y 8239 MAR	Y 8284 BEZ	Y 8329 BEZ
Y 8240 BEZ	Y 8285 NAN	Y 8330 MET
Y 8241 LON	Y 8286 LEN	Y 8331 LEN
Y 8242 ACH	Y 8287 TOU	Y 8332 MET
Y 8243 LEN	Y 8288 LIM	Y 8333 TSP
Y 8244 MET	Y 8289 LIM	Y 8334 PLV
Y 8245 REN	Y 8290 LEN	Y 8335 PLV
Y 8246 NAN	Y 8291 NEV	Y 8336 PLV
Y 8247 SOT	Y 8292 LIM	Y 8337 NEV
Y 8248 REN	Y 8293 CBY	Y 8338 MAR
Y 8249 REN	Y 8294 LYV	Y 8339 LYV
Y 8250 SOT	Y 8295 NEV	Y 8340
Y 8251 REN	Y 8296 TSP	Y 8341 CBY
Y 8252 ACH	Y 8297 STN	Y 8342 BOR
Y 8253 SOT	Y 8298 LIM	Y 8343 TSP
Y 8254 ACH	Y 8299 NEV	Y 8344
Y 8255 SOT	Y 8300 LON	Y 8345
Y 8256 CBY	Y 8301 CBY	Y 8346 SOT
Y 8257 DIJ	Y 8302 MAR	Y 8347 CBY
Y 8258 CBY	Y 8303 NEV	Y 8348 TSP
Y 8259 BOR	Y 8304 BOR	Y 8349
Y 8260 LYV	Y 8305 LEN	Y 8350
Y 8261 LEN	Y 8306 ACH	Y 8351

Y 8352	Y 8379	Y 8405
Y 8353	Y 8380	Y 8406
Y 8354	Y 8381	Y 8407
Y 8355	Y 8382	Y 8408
Y 8356	Y 8383	Y 8409
Y 8357	Y 8384	Y 8410
Y 8358	Y 8385	Y 8411
Y 8359 TSP	Y 8386	Y 8412
Y 8360	Y 8387	Y 8413
Y 8361	Y 8388	Y 8414
Y 8362 BOR	Y 8389	Y 8415
Y 8363	Y 8390	Y 8416
Y 8364	Y 8391	Y 8417
Y 8365	Y 8392	Y 8418
Y 8366	Y 8393	Y 8419
Y 8367	Y 8394	Y 8420
Y 8368 BOR	Y 8395	Y 8421
Y 8369	Y 8396	Y 8422
Y 8370	Y 8397	Y 8423
Y 8371	Y 8398	Y 8424
Y 8372	Y 8399	Y 8425
Y 8373	Y 8400	Y 8426
Y 8374	Y 8401 LEN	Y 8427
Y 8375	Y 8402	Y 8428
Y 8376	Y 8403	Y 8429
Y 8377	Y 8404	Y 8430
Y 8378		

NARROW GAUGE LOCOMOTIVES

CHEMIN DE FER BLANC-ARGENT

BUZANÇAIS - SALBRIS LINE

Although owned by the SNCF, this line is operated by the above company.

Gauge: 1000 mm.
Depot & Works: Romorantin.

T11 CLASS   C

Built: 1940-41 by CFD Neuillé Pont Pierre.
Engine: Willème 517F8 of 132 kW (175 hp).
Transmission: Mechanical.
Weight: 16 tonnes.
Length: 6.00 m (19 ft 8 in).
Maximum Speed: 30 km/h (19 mph).

T11   T12

T13 CLASS   C

Built: 1953 by CFD Périguex.
Engine: Willème 517F8 of 132 kW (175 hp).
Transmission: Mechanical.
Weight: 17 tonnes.
Length: 8.45 m (27 ft 9 in).
Maximum Speed: 30 km/h (19 mph).

T13   T14

CHEMINS DE FER DE LA CORSE

CORSICA RAILWAYS

Gauge: 1000 mm.
Depot & Works: Cassamozza.

1 C

Built: 1948 by CFD Montmirail.
Engine: 150 kW (200 hp).
Transmission: Mechanical.
Weight: tonnes.
Length: m (ft in).
Maximum Speed: km/h (mph).

1

2 C

Built: 1951 by VFD Vizille.
Engine: 150 kW (200 hp).
Transmission: Mechanical.
Weight: tonnes.
Length: m (ft in).
Maximum Speed: km/h (mph).

2

3 C-1

Built: 1948 by SE Cosne.
Engine: 150 kW (200 hp).
Transmission: Mechanical.
Weight: tonnes.
Length: m (ft in).
Maximum Speed: km/h (mph).

3

114 B-2

Built: 1955 at Bastia Works. (Rebuilt from railcar built 1938).
Engine: 112 kW (150 hp).
Transmission: Mechanical.
Weight: tonnes.
Length: m (ft in).
Maximum Speed: km/h (mph).

114

401 CLASS   Bo-Bo

Built: 1951 by B & L.
Engine: 450 kW (600 hp).
Transmission: Electric.
Weight: tonnes.
Length: m (ft in).
Maximum Speed: km/h (mph).

401

403   B

Built: 1956 at Bastia Works. (Built on power bogie of railcar 103).
Engine: 157 kW (210 hp).
Transmission: Mechanical.
Weight: tonnes.
Length: m (ft in).
Maximum Speed: km/h (mph).

403

404 CLASS   B

Built: 1963 by CFD Montmirail.
Engine: 310 kW (410 hp).
Transmission: Hydraulic.
Weight: tonnes.
Length: m (ft in).
Maximum Speed: km/h (mph).

404   405

401 CLASS (Continued)   Bo-Bo

413

Top: SNCF Y 7400 class no. Y 7731 at Paris La Plaine Depot on 21.02.88.
(R. G. Morris)

Bottom: Blanc Argent Ligne no. 14 at Valencenay on 30.12.88. *(D. Rowland)*

PRIVATE RAILWAYS

Chemins de Fer de la Provence

Gauge: 1000 mm.
Line: Nice Gare du Sud - Digne (151 km).
Depots: Digne, Nice, Puget-Théniers.
Works: Lingostière.

DIESEL LOCOMOTIVES

51   D

Built: 1934 by CFD Montmirail.
Engine: 150 kW (200 hp).
Transmission: Mechanical.
Weight: tonnes.   **Length:**   m (ft in).
Maximum   Speed: km/h (mph).

51

62   B-B

Built: 1951 by B & L.
Engine: 450 kW (600 hp).
Transmission: Electric.
Weight: tonnes.   **Length:**   m (ft in).
Maximum   Speed: km/h (mph).

62

BB401 CLASS   B-B

Built: 1938 (*1948) by CFD Montmirail.
Engine: 310 kW (410 hp).
Transmission: Mechanical.
Weight: tonnes.   **Length:**   m (ft in).
Maximum   Speed: km/h (mph).

BB 401   BB 402

STEAM LOCOMOTIVES

E 327 4-6-0T

Built: 1909 by Fives-Lille.
Boiler Pressure:
Cylinders:
Weight: tonnes.
Length: m (ft in).
Maximum Speed: km/h (mph).

E 327

E 211 2-4-6-0T

Built: 1891 by Henschel.
Boiler Pressure:
Cylinders:
Weight: tonnes.
Length: m (ft in).
Maximum Speed: km/h (mph).

E 211

CHEMIN DE FER DE CHAMONIX AU MONTENVERS

Gauge: 1000 mm - Rack System.
Line: Chamonix - Montenvers (6 km).
Depot: St. Gervais.

31 CLASS 1-B

Built: 1967 (*1972) by SLM.
Engine: Poyaud A12-150Se of 485 kW (640 hp).
Transmission: Hydraulic.
Weight: 23.3 tonnes.   **Length:** 7.5 m (24 ft 7 in).
Maximum Speed: 21 km/h (13 mph).

31   32   33